TURNING
FERAL

TURNING FERAL

A Modern Journey of Hunting,
Trapping, and Living Intentionally
in the Wilderness

ZACHARY CRAIG HANSON

LIONCREST
PUBLISHING

TURNING FERAL
A Modern Journey of Hunting, Trapping, and Living Intentionally in the Wilderness

ISBN   978-1-5445-3516-6   *Hardcover*

978-1-5445-3517-3   *Paperback*

978-1-5445-3518-0   *Ebook*

CONTENTS

For my children.
May you always feel supported to follow your dreams,
no matter how insurmountable or crazy they may seem.

ACKNOWLEDGMENTS

Writing a publishable book is hard. It's even harder when you have a one-year-old daughter and another child on the way, live in a remote cabin, and work a demanding full-time job that you must juggle while learning to hunt and trap. Writing this book took many mornings of waking up at 3:00 a.m. to get a few hours in before my daily chores and work meetings, but it often bled into and took precedence over my other responsibilities.

Without my amazing wife Olesya's help, this book would have never seen the light of day. She picked up the slack in all of the areas where I would frequently drop the ball and was a source of steady encouragement day in and day out. Not once did she complain when I missed bath time with the baby, or when I had to check my traplines before bed, or when I'd come inside covered in animal bits only to sit at my laptop and write "just a little more."

Olesya, you are my rock and best friend, and I thank you so much for your support. I love you.

A very special thanks is also due to our friend and childcare guru, Cindy Inama. After watching our rambunctious toddler during the day, she patiently sat with me over a series of weeks and listened to me read my book out loud, cover to cover. Her feedback, tears, and encouragement gave me the strength to get this book over the finish line. Thank you for all you do for our family, Cindy!

To everyone on the Scribe team in Austin, Texas, thank you for your support along the way. The writing methods I learned and was able to refine have made me a much better author and a genuinely better human being. Thanks to Tucker Max for pushing me to think more deeply about my subject matter, to Chas Hoppe for poking holes in my story line, and Hussein Al-Baiaty for checking in on my progress! I also want to thank my publishing manager for helping coordinate all of the intricate and time-sensitive steps that came after submitting my manuscript, along with the rest of the team who helped me refine my story through multiple rounds of editing, title workshopping, and of course, coming up with great cover art. Thank you all from the bottom of my heart.

To the digital mentors that inspired me on my hunting and trapping adventures, thank you. A special hat tip goes out to Clay Newcomb of MeatEater, Tom Miranda of Lazy CK Ranch, and Rusty Kramer of the Idaho Trappers Association. They were open to my cold emails and selflessly reviewed the chapters where I mentioned them, giving me more encouragement to finish this work than they will ever know.

I want to thank all of the people in our remote Idaho town who entered my life at a tumultuous time in my personal story. You all helped pull me out of the shell I was living in, and I can't thank you enough for your friendship. To Gene Haught, thank you for being a friend and for pushing me to get proper backcountry training, which may well have saved my wife's life, as well as a big thank you for all of the help you and Jules provide for our town day in and day out.

Lastly, to my buddies Alex Cowdry, Diogo Ribeiro, Blake McClellan, Eric Becker, and Kyle Zibrowski who came out to visit and spend time exploring the woods with me, thank you for your friendship. It's what makes these explorations of self-improvement worth it, as you all push me to be a better and more well-rounded person.

INTRODUCTION

In trapper parlance, I had just conducted a perfect front-paw high-pad catch in my American-made four-coil spring-steel wolf trap—an achievement I had been after for years. My elation only lasted for a fraction of a second, though, as my intestines began to twist at the realization that I had captured a non-target species.

Almost instantaneously, a few more synapses in my brain fired off, and I began to feel the cold steel on my wrist. As blood rushed from every part of my body to the impact site, I could feel and hear my own heartbeat in the dead silence of the snowy December day. The pain around my wrist began to set in, and so did the gravity of my situation.

The wolf trap I'd been setting was engineered to hold an unhappy ultrapredator canine and could only be released by sheer strength or a specialized setting tool. Lacking in the one-handed strength department, my fate rested in that magical device to free my now-swelling hand. But sadly, the setting tool that I so desperately needed was back at my cabin, a blustery five miles away over rough terrain.

The "oh-shit algebra" that was going on in my head quickly turned into a complex differential equation as I realized there was no cell phone service and I could not call for help. I was on my own. With the sun beginning to set, fresh snow falling, and temperatures forecasted to dip below zero, I realized that if I couldn't get out of the woods and back to my cabin, there was a real possibility I could die.

I did my best to gather my equipment, cranked my snowmobile with my nondominant hand, and looked down at the painful metal bracelet I was wearing. Yet I couldn't help but smile. Why? Well, despite the hard lesson I was learning about treating every trap with caution, I was out working my wolf trapline in some of the most beautiful country on earth, pursuing a lost art that was rehabilitating me.

I was living life the way I wanted to. A life that hearkened back to the 1800s and followed the patterns set by the tough men and women who founded our country. Pioneers, like me, who were drawn to the West for gold, fur, and promises of a better life. Though there probably wasn't much gold left "in them thar hills," there was plenty of passion left in the Western identity, "the call of the wild," and the desire to build a better life.

You see, before I locked onto the lust-filled gaze of the Rocky Mountains, I had spent the last decade building a lucrative career in artificial intelligence. As part of that veneer of success, I had done everything I could to keep up with the Joneses—the nice house, respected career, new cars, exotic vacations—yet somehow I still felt hollow.

I'd been going through life on cruise control. On some subconscious level, I'd known that the suburban life path I'd been on wasn't for me, so I would find ways to challenge myself just to feel alive. I pursued jiu-jitsu at a high level, ran ultramarathons, regularly tried new diets, and even sought out higher-level education, but no activity or challenge I undertook seemed to cure the numbness I felt deep in my soul.

In order to replenish my shriveled sense of self and masculinity, I decided to take the bull by the horns and set out on a quest to experience life in its rawest form. I sought a life that would carry true hardship and consequence. One that would require daily discipline to chop wood for warmth, hunt to provide food, and trap furs for clothing. And now I was getting it all—in spades.

With my hand throbbing in that wolf trap, temperatures dropping, and a pained smile on my face, I was finally up against the consequences of my actions that I'd been looking for. And in that moment my soul was full.

Living on My Own Terms

The trap that gripped me was cold and tangible, but the trap of my former suburban life had also felt cold and unrelenting. My path toward suburban sedation, however, was not intentional but a culmination of many uncontrollable factors. Coming out of college, I was hit hard by the great recession, the proliferation of social media, and a need for validation by achieving the same suburban American Dream that my parents and grandparents had attained. With few jobs to be had in the United States for an inexperienced college graduate during the recession, I ended up working for several years overseas for low pay until I was able to elbow my way into a career at a large technology corporation back stateside.

Once I had established myself as a hard worker, I made a few strategic internal moves to get into a role in the US job market that focused on a growing area of study, artificial intelligence (AI). In that new role, I helped architect many of the products that had a net-negative effect on the world. Things such as infinite scrolling, "like" functionality, ad optimization, and other attention-diverting AI features that are commonplace in the digital products we use every day. I took pride in my work and also in earning a paycheck big enough to start building my own suburban dream.

Unknowingly, however, I was helping to build the very products that would tear down the "white-picket-fence life" I had fought so hard to architect. It started slowly, but the products I was helping to build for the masses also became an omnipresent feature in our own suburban lives. In a Shakespearean way, my career in AI and immersion in social media directly contributed to the failure of my first marriage. And the subsequent turbulence of that experience opened my eyes to the fact that my generation lives life through an unrealistic filter and that the American Dream of my parents' and grandparents' generation, the very thing I had been fighting for, was *dead*.

I found myself sitting at a crossroads looking at the trajectory of our world through the lens of technology and pining for real, undoctored, unfiltered experiences that were in short supply.

This ultimately led me to my own unique and fulfilling way of life deep in the backwoods of North America.

If you have picked up this book, then you, too, are likely someone trying to shed the dead skin of a modern career, a failing relationship, or technological dependency and are seeking to experience life on your own terms.

I hope my stories of wrestling with my own identity, morality, and personal limitations as I learned to hunt, trap, and build a more sustainable life will be an inspiration for those seeking to cut through the digital noise of the twenty-first century and rediscover what's truly meaningful.

PART I

INTO THE WILD

Find out who you are and do it on purpose.

—DOLLY PARTON

1

TRAPPED

Two minutes before my alarm sounded at 3:15 a.m., my eyes opened to the low, blue hue coming from my wife's iPhone, an omnipresent feature in our all-too-connected lives. Clearing the sleep from my eyes, I caught a glimpse of the doom scrolling as her thumb whizzed past photoshopped influencers showcasing their extravagant lifestyles near and afar.

Without saying a word, I mentally ran through my plan of execution for the day. Like every Monday, I needed to shower, make coffee, and get in the car by 3:45 a.m. to make it to the New Orleans International Airport for my weekly flight to Washington, DC. If all went well, I would be in our company's swanky "innovation lab," brimming with free snacks, by no later than 10:00 a.m.

After two minutes of swirling thoughts, my alarm went off like the starting gun at a track meet. I then commenced my highly choreographed morning dance.

Morning Samba

Rolling out of our intentionally stiff therapeutic mattress, I plodded to the bathroom where my prestarched uniform awaited in my prepacked Tumi suitcase—trousers, button-down shirt, sport coat, Cole Haan shoes, and the one glimmer of individuality in the whole getup: socks stitched with the words "this meeting sucks," which I'd picked up at a tech conference earlier that year in Zurich.

The dripping water and steam on the glass door of our shower gave the clothes a *Clockwork Orange* aesthetic, with colors and fabrics bleeding together. I began to think about how much I hated the uncomfortable, too-tight pants, the restricting shoes, and the narrow-shoulder feel of my sport coat.

Recognizing those negative thoughts, I refocused my attention on the shower itself, feeling the water wash over me—just as I had been taught to do in a mindfulness course I'd taken years earlier. But my mind wandered again, this time to a pattern in the tile that only I could see: a splash of color and texture that looked to me like an ancient Neanderthal holding a spear.

It got me thinking about the life I had previously lived: a revolution in Kyrgyzstan, long nights on the outskirts of Paris, and riding out the Arab Spring in the deserts of Saudi Arabia—an adventurous life I had traded for this domestication.

Once again I refocused on the task at hand, suppressed my thoughts, and went on with my ritual morning dance. Punctuality was my religion. I grabbed one of our plush, high-thread-count towels and stepped out into the cold. Toweling off, I looked into the "his" mirror above our granite vanity and took a deep, conscious breath before grabbing the first piece of my corporate straightjacket. Piece by piece, I sealed my fate for the week, and once the last button was fastened, I grabbed my suitcase. With a silent goodbye to my now-sleeping wife and dogs, I headed off to the kitchen.

I worked my way around the counter island and shuffled through a drawer to find a bag of our fair-trade, whole-bean coffee that arrived fresh at our door every month. I poured a handful of dark, oily beans into the coffee grinder and hit the pulse button for the perfect grind. As I tamped the grounds into the espresso filter, I thought about how relatable the coffee was, grown and harvested on some family farm in Peru. I imagined that I, too, was meant to be closer to the source of something, wherever that source may be.

As the slow drip of coffee began to wane, I snapped back to reality. With my home-brewed coffee in hand, the next steps in my Monday-morning samba began.

I walked through our high-ceiling foyer and opened the heavy, ten-foot-tall front door, stepping out into the humid south Louisiana morning. Our antique gas lanterns cast flickering light on the morning dew beginning to collect on our perfectly manicured lawn. I took pride in that lawn and breathed in the fresh smell of grass, thinking of how I would have to cut it again soon, or the homeowners association would be on my back about it. I wrestled my phone out of my tight pants pocket, got into the car, connected to Bluetooth, and cued up a podcast. I had one hour to get to the airport—ritualistic time I used to get coached by any number of stoic podcasters, silently convincing myself that *this* was a life well lived. A life that was easy, luxurious, and fraught with *zero* peril.

My phone buzzed, notifying me that my first-class upgrade had finally been approved, a byproduct of all the time I'd spent gaming the airline point system. Knowing that I would now get a nice breakfast with real silverware in just over two hours, I backed out of the driveway and headed south like a drone.

Waking Up

The eighty miles of flatland between my home and the airport were blanketed by dark bayou waters that gave a macabre and gothic feel to the early morning. With limited mental bandwidth needed to focus on the empty road, my mind began to wander again. I thought about the aquatic creatures that live in the waters just beyond the old oak trees covered with Spanish moss, and how they represented a fear I held in the depths of my subconscious—a fear of the true violence of nature.

I reached the airport parking lot and involuntarily began to curse. Someone with an out-of-state license plate had brazenly taken *my* usual parking spot, forcing me into an uncovered area at the top of the garage. This taxed my sense of entitlement too early in the morning.

I arrived at my gate and chatted with Tom, a McKinsey consultant, asking if his daughter had started jiu-jitsu classes at the gym I'd suggested. I then turned to my regular seatmate, Donna Brazile, former chairwoman of the Democratic National Committee, to see how her kitchen renovation was going. I was part of a small club of people that traveled with enough frequency to get into our first-class, frequent-fliers group. I believed my own hype that I had "made it" and forcefully framed this experience in my psyche as a sign of a fulfilled and well-lived life. Once seated, our stewardess brought me my black coffee in a ceramic mug, and I tried to look busy and studious, reading some in-vogue business book.

We taxied to the end of the tarmac and pointed northward. As our plane started to gain altitude, I began to count the power lines that cut directly across Lake Pontchartrain before I opened my laptop, planning to diligently work on a presentation for the remainder of the flight. Yet my willpower to do actual work was short-lived. I opened an alternate tab in my web browser and started to search for swanky bars in New York and Washington, DC. My time that week would be split between those two cities, and I needed to host social meetups for each team I visited. With company money not an issue, I landed on a few different options and emailed my libation-friendly colleagues to see which locations they preferred.

Yet my excitement for these get-togethers dampened as I suddenly remembered a recent trip home from New York City that was bookended by delayed travel. That delay had forced me to conduct a "happy hour" with a few colleagues in the dingy TGI Friday's deep in the bowels of Penn Station, which had opened my eyes to how much I genuinely dislike those social functions.

As I closed on the bar reservations for the week, the pilot's voice came over the speaker to let us know we would soon be landing at Ronald Reagan International Airport. I decided to disconnect my brain for the remainder of the flight and turned on one of my favorite childhood movies, *Jeremiah Johnson,* a classic mountain-man tale starring Robert Redford that I'd seen many times. I keyed into a scene where Redford's character, Jeremiah, converses with a fellow mountain man, Del Gue. Del recalls how his "pap" and "mam" tried to discourage him from leaving the norms of society to become a mountain man living among "animals" and "savages." But Del insists that the Rocky Mountains are "the marrow of the world."

These words were destined to change the trajectory of my life. They plowed into my soul and watered a seed that had known nothing but drought for more than a decade.

I stared westward through the plane window and thought about the shallow pride I took in so many frivolous things. I possessed no skills for surviving anywhere but in the corporate world. I had never killed or processed my own food, had never grown a garden, and couldn't even change my own car oil. I was a pawn, dependent on a frail system to support my own family's survival in this world.

With hollow eyes, I caught a glimpse of the traffic buzzing around our nation's capital as we began to land. I couldn't help but imagine that I was looking into a terrarium, and the mass of cars and bodies were just like ants acting and moving out of habit more than desire—precisely as I had done since waking up that morning.

As our plane made contact with the earth once again, it was finally dawning on me that I was utterly trapped in a life I didn't really want.

2

TARGET PRACTICE

Jeremiah Johnson's need to escape the norms of society by retreating to the Rockies stuck with me throughout the entire workweek in our country's largest metropolitan cities. My mind wandered to places in the Rocky Mountains I had never been and to hard-earned experiences I had never actually had. I relied on technology to get *anything* done in those large cities. For example, if I needed to go just a few blocks away, it took one click, and an Uber would pull up to my location. If I wanted food, DoorDash would bring it to me. And when I needed to satisfy my mental wanderlust for an alternative lifestyle, I would just scroll through a celebrity hunter's Instagram account.

These feelings of wanting to break free weren't entirely new to me. They had actually begun in childhood.

Dormant Ember

As a young kid, I had always felt that somehow I'd been born in the wrong era. I would devour any historical book I could find about the hard lives lived out West—the stories of Lewis and Clark, Sacagawea, Jim Bridger, and John Colter; men and women who could endure extreme loss, unforgiving winters, and continuous war. The type of people who, when things got tough, would just put their heads down, gnaw on some willow bark, and persevere no matter what.

Yet slowly over the years, these interests of mine had eroded to occupy only the smallest corner of my brain. Society, my career, and my family had coached me into believing that a mountain man's life was not something to seek. Those ways of the West were over. We were now a cultured and domesticated civilization that sought higher education and stable jobs and needed to procreate just so our kids could repeat the same cycle.

Still, Jeremiah Johnson and Del Gue lingered with me, an ember of living a tough and rugged life outdoors, waiting to erupt into flame. That fateful week in Washington, DC, was a turning point. The dormant embers of my childhood dreams started to burn into a wildfire that took hold so quickly and consumed so many acres in my consciousness that as soon as I got home, I made a plan to get a taste of the life that my childhood heroes had lived.

Bow and Quiver

Not knowing where to begin my journey, I sought a mental escape in the Instagram influencers who practiced archery hunting, while I navigated the concrete jungles of different cities week in and week out. The idea of chasing animals through tall brush with a bow and quiver of arrows seemed romantic to me. This was reinforced by an ill-conceived notion that archery was more "noble" than rifle hunting, as it gave the animal a fairer chance. With not much thought, I decided to take up the sport of archery and hunting in order to provide a supplemental and decidedly healthier food source for my family—a notion that my wife found quite comical.

Yet once her laughter stopped and she laid out the rationale for why this was such a silly idea, I remained resolute. Yes, the odds were stacked against me. I didn't come from a hunting family, and I had absolutely no clue about how to get started. I could not tell the difference between a deer's nose or asshole, but what I lacked in know-how, I would make up for in grit and determination.

Wasting no time, I started to phone in favors to childhood friends who hunted. After a few calls, I was able to find someone in my extended circle of friends who was of similar size and build to me. It took some convincing, but I was able to get him to sell me my first used compound bow, an old hand-me-down with fraying strings, wooden handles, and a draw length that was just a little too short for me.

I am not a natural talent at sports, and I take a bit longer than most to get the hang of new skills. So, knowing my new bow was on the way fueled some of my internal anxiety about potential embarrassment. I decided to build an archery range in our backyard *behind* our tall fence so I could fine-tune my shooting skills between my work's Zoom call meetings, and away from prying eyes.

After finding some rough schematics online, I went to Home Depot to get supplies. A few sweaty and angst-filled hours later, I had almost completed building a respectable twenty-five yard practice range. The only thing left to do was to carry a large cross-beam with two heavy horse-stall mats attached to it across our yard. I'd then have to hoist the beam and anchor it to two vertical posts that I had already installed in concrete. By necessity, I was already becoming handier. But getting that crossbeam and its thick rubber skirt across the yard was more of a chore than I had anticipated. In the hot Louisiana sun, I put it across my back and began pulling off my own rendition of *The Passion of the Christ*.

One foot in front of the other, I slowly tugged, dragged, and prayed that I would be able to get the cross that I bore into place. I spent the next two hours engineering ways to lift the beam into its final resting spot to complete my first archery range, all while my wife watched with a giggle from our air-conditioned living room.

Backyard archery range.

Once completed, I thought that my hardest efforts were out of the way. That was until my bow arrived a few days later, when the real struggle began.

I couldn't even pull back the string. The ensuing hours of YouTube how-to videos did nothing to help as I tried to figure out the knack of getting my bow drawn back. I was left sore, sweaty, demoralized, and pissed off. It took two days before I finally, by accident, got my seventy-pound draw bow pulled back. This success caught me so off guard that I immediately committed a cardinal archery sin and "dry fired" my bow. With no arrow on the rest, my string slammed into the rubber stoppers, making a god-awful twanging sound that sent a shock wave through my left arm and released the already loose grip I had on my bowels.

Only later would I find out that this rookie error could have rendered my bow immediately useless, or worse, that I could have sustained serious injury to my face and body had my bow decided to explode into tiny fragments. With ignorance as my only friend, and with no injuries or a broken bow, I patted myself on the back and loaded my first arrow.

The kinetic energy I felt in the string as I attached a four-hundred-grain death-dart to it was enlivening—even if my arms and bow were wobbling around like Forrest Gump's legs during the first steps in his magic shoes. As I looked down my twenty-five-yard range and punched the trigger on my release, fear of the unknown took over. I instinctively closed my eyes and waited until I heard the unmistakable thwack of an arrow finding its target.

Of course, my arrow cruised a good two feet above the brightly colored target bag I was aiming for and embedded itself into the wooden upper crossbeam that I had wrestled into place just a week before. Whoops.

Still, in that moment, I felt all was right with the world. I was far from being deadly (at least to an animal, though the personal safety of myself and my neighbors was a different story). But I was out there, and I had crossed the first hurdle on my path toward learning what it meant to be a twenty-first-century mountain man. In the months that followed, I would constantly be at my range between work calls, fiddling with different techniques and slowly growing some confidence in my shooting ability.

As my confidence snowballed, I decided to invite my close friend and new archery buddy, Alex, to my range to practice together.

Heckling Session

Alex and I were part of a "husbands club" of sorts, as both of our wives were FBI special agents. We had become close after finding out that we both had an interest in learning to hunt as adults and proving to ourselves that we could provide food for our families if we ever needed to.

Our wives would talk shop about any number of disturbing domestic security issues at our frequent dinner parties, while we would sneak off to shoot our bows and talk about all of the hunts we wanted to do in the future. At some point in one of our conversations, we discussed how confident we were both feeling with our practice and openly wondered if we would be able to perform when it came time to actually harvest an animal. We had both read about the hunting phenomenon called "buck fever," when hunters lose their composure under the pressure of coming face-to-face with an animal and miss seemingly simple shots. This concerned us, given the static nature of our practice.

On the spot, we decided that we needed to introduce some stress and anxiety into our shot routines to help mimic the fear we might face when we got into the woods. Our bright idea, with the help of a bottle or two of red wine, was to bring our wives— both trained interrogators and hostage negotiators—to heckle us during our next practice round. We figured that no deer or animal would ever be able to demean and poke at our core insecurities like our wives, and boy were we right.

Getting heckled by some FBI special agents.

The second we stood on that shooting platform with two stone-faced women behind us, we could feel our blood pressure rise. After my first shot went a bit wide, the insults and questions came in hot.

"Really, Zach? Did you even try?"

"Well, that was money well spent. You do know that you are *actually* supposed to hit the target, right?"

"Bambi's mom shouldn't be too concerned at this point."

"Nice try, sweetie. I guess we'll all just starve to death during the apocalypse."

It was truly hard to recompose and block out the words. However, taking a moment to get fully Zen and leverage the same meditation tricks I had used to drudge through pointless work days pulled me back on target.

With this heckling session in the bag and our egos checked, Alex and I were feeling pretty high on the hog regarding our slow evolution from gatherers to marginally passable hunters. It was a start, but there was so much more to learn.

3

HOG WILD

By the time I had shot close to a thousand arrows, which I kept track of with an Excel spreadsheet, I was hitting the target every time. I could now walk into my backyard range and know with certainty that I would not lodge an arrow in my fence or have to pull out my ladder and binoculars to scour my neighbors rooftops for protruding arrows.

I felt that I could move on to the next phase of my harebrained scheme and actually hunt. Still knowing nothing about nothing, I turned to the internet to learn all about what it would take to get a hunting license and an archery permit, and also to figure out the details of seasons, times, and places to pull this off. I was beginning to get overwhelmed by the sheer magnitude of all that is involved in the process of legally hunting when I stumbled across a website for an "outfitter" from southern Arkansas.

Pig Hunting

Our would-be guide was just an eight-hour drive away and claimed to run an outfit for wild-hog hunting that would cost only two hundred dollars for a whole weekend. There was no licensing needed since it was on his own private land. With little forethought, my love for bacon and my inner tightwad took over, and I called this guy up. After a short conversation, he reassured me that this was all legal and convinced me to sign Alex and me up for a weekend of archery pig hunting.

We had no idea what to expect, but we packed up what little ragtag gear we had recently collected and drove north. The outfitter mentioned that once we heard banjos in the mid-October air, we would know we were close, and he wasn't lying. At dusk on a Friday afternoon, we pulled into a little homestead that was over thirty miles from the nearest Walmart or Waffle House, a feat that is hard to accomplish in the southern United States and speaks to the remoteness of the property.

On arrival, we were met with the requisite amount of southern hospitality and treated to a dinner of wild pork loin with our host and his family. We chatted about the influx of feral pigs, how they decimate family crops every year, and how harvesting these animals was helpful to the local agricultural economy. Our host even joked about paying us if we had ample success, and judging by the taxidermy that adorned their home, there were plenty of big boars to be found.We closed dinner with a prayer for our success, an act that took my atheist buddy by surprise, and were told to be ready with our bows by 4:00 a.m.

The next morning, we awoke to a cold and wet day. After grabbing our gear, we each hopped on a four-wheeler with our intrepid and near-toothless hosts and headed into the woods. Alex was riding shotgun on a four-wheeler with our host's wife, while I was seated behind the lead patriarch on another four-wheeler, trying not to hold on too tightly to his beer belly as we sped away. As the cold air rushed down the back of my camouflage sweatshirt, I could hear our host yell out to me over the sound of the engine that he had never hosted bowhunters before, and he hoped we would be good shots when the time came.

I made some witty reply steeped in false confidence, and when we reached the deep woods, he killed the engine and quickly removed my loving embrace from his waist. The silence of the predawn deep woods consumed us. He pointed me to my tree stand that was several hundred meters away from where Alex was staging, gestured to an automated corn feeder where I should expect the pigs to come, and said, "Good luck."

That was the only advice I received on my first-ever hunt. Before I could ask any questions, he was gone. With just me, my inexperience, and bow, I decided to tackle my first problem: climbing the tree stand. The mechanics of a tree stand may seem obvious, but having never hunted, much less from a tree stand, I was at a loss.

In a normal situation, you would hoist your weapon up to the top of the tree with a rope, attach your safety harness to the tree, and climb to the top using both hands on the ladder. In my case, I had no safety harness and no instruction, and I decided that my best bet was to climb the ladder to the top with one hand while holding my bow in the other. The higher I got, the more I could feel my bones instinctively pressing into the hardwood.

I was climbing with four points of contact and had my bow wedged between my thighs and chest, which forced me into a weird aerial fetal position. Once at the top, it took me twenty minutes just to turn myself around and get settled in my chair. After finally sitting down, I became unsure if I would even be able to draw my bow while sitting that high in the air. With no safety harness, it seemed that shooting at such a steep angle would be impossible compared to the flat-land shooting I had practiced.

Sitting uncomfortably high in my first tree stand in Arkansas.

Putting my fears and worries aside for a brief second, I found that a smile had crept onto my face with the realization that this was the culmination of months of embarrassing and hard work. I was now in position for my first kill, filled with testosterone, and excited for some action.

The adrenaline gods were continually kind to me on this trip and would occasionally visit and rewarm my body at odd intervals. Every crunch of a leaf, bark of a squirrel, or breeze would send my brain into overdrive, trying to calculate which direction I might see a pig walk in from. I was on high alert, and I had never been more still or concentrated in my life.

In the lead-up to this hunt, I had every scenario planned in my head and a game plan as to how I would react. I knew exactly how I would silently load an arrow, attach my release, adjust my sight, and follow through on a perfectly executed and ethical kill shot. With all of this mental planning, however, I had failed to prepare myself for the most important and likely scenario: nothing.

For hours I sat, froze, and thought. Nothing moved, nothing materialized in front of my eyes, and not one of the scenarios I had fantasized about became a reality. For eight hours I sat in that tree, expecting to have my first experience in taking an animal's life for food...and then the sun set.

Crawling down from my tetanus-laden tree stand, I walked over to see Alex. We swapped stories of sounds we heard throughout the day and started to psych ourselves up for our second and last day of hunting. We got back to the "lodge," warmed up, ate, and plotted an even earlier wakeup call for the last hunting day.

At four o'clock the next morning, our hosts were already ferrying us to our respective stands. It was hard to believe, but that morning was even colder than the last, and I was already anticipating the uncontrollable shivers that I knew were on the way. With no one there to witness my juggling act, I once again clambered up my tree and settled in for what I just knew would be the day that I would harvest my first animal.

However, despite my best intentions, this day played out just as the one before. A cruel lesson to learn as a hunting adult was that this sport was hard, cold, and generally really boring. If truth be told, by midday, I was counting the squirrels in nearby trees and debating whether I should try to hit one with an arrow, just to say I had harvested *something*. But as the sun once again began to set on another unsuccessful day, the woods had a parting gift for me.

As I stood on my wobbly platform preparing to go meet Alex, I heard the most god-awful screech rip through the treetops. I am not a cowardly individual, but for someone who had not spent a ton of time alone in the woods, I would be a liar if I said that adrenaline didn't ooze out of my eyeballs in that moment. Without hesitation, I did what most twenty-first-century city dwellers do when faced with an unknown threat in the dark: I turned on my iPhone light.

In a feeble attempt to cast a comforting light out into the darkness, I sat there with my phone and listened to that echoing screech. To my dismay, it was getting louder and closer, and my cortisol levels continued to rise. My untrained ear could only compare the deep yet shrill whooping sound to a wild primate, and when you are out of your element, your brain will play out irrational scenarios. In my mind's eye, I was envisioning a pissed-off baboon that was somehow on the loose from a local zoo, swinging through the treetops, on its way to rip my face off with one hairy hand.

In a rush, I practically fell down my tree to go find Alex. When our iPhone lights met in the woods, we both shared the universal facial expression of "what in the hell was that?" With the hair raised on the back of our necks, we quickly followed the trail out of the woods and back to the relative safety of the paved road where our hosts were waiting for us, right on time for the ride back to their homestead.

As I would come to learn over the next few years, most things that go bump in the night are not the threat they seem. Over our departing dinner with our hosts, I got up the courage to ask if there was a zoo nearby or if anything could make the noise of a baboon in the vicinity. Without missing a beat, our hosts began to chuckle at the hair-raising description of the noise we had encountered. With their cutting laughs, I knew that my back-woods tormenter had to be something benign. They explained that the common barred owl makes a distinctive yet horrifying mating call that fit my description to a tee.

Embarrassed, tired, and with no game meat to put in the cool-ers we had purchased, my comrade Alex and I packed our bags and headed home to relay the stories of our incompetency to our increasingly skeptical wives.

4

A TASTE OF BLOOD

Despite our woes, the ride home from our failed inaugural hunt was filled with optimism. Alex and I chatted about the steep learning curve we were on and what may lay ahead of us in our hunting lives. We jointly fantasized about one day hunting large elk in the Rockies or potentially chasing antelope across the Western Plains.

Impressively, all of this excitement and mental wanderlust came about from sitting in a tree, shivering uncontrollably for eight hours, and not seeing a damn thing other than some neurotic squirrels. That weekend in Arkansas had seen a shift in our identities. Our long dormant, primal spirits were now wide awake and, quite frankly, would not shut up. Our souls were screaming at us that we were now providers, even if we had not seen success yet.

Answering that spiritual call, we started to plot what was next in our hunting journey. We decided to focus on a larger game animal this time around, one that is pervasive in the southeastern United States: the white-tailed deer. Lucky for us, my wife's family *was* a hunting family, and they lived in one of the white-tailed deer meccas of the United States, Middle Tennessee.

Her family was an amazing group when it came to hunting—something I had not appreciated about them until I started my own explorations into this subculture. They were all sustenance hunters and used deer meat, wild birds, and even squirrels to augment their grocery-buying habits every year.

Yes, I said squirrel. Every year, her large family would host an annual squirrel hunt, an event that became so popular that the Tennessee Wildlife Resources Agency got involved to help sponsor it. Teams of four would sign up to hunt the local woods, while volunteers back at base camp would raffle off prizes and do youth hunting education courses. Though I had attended the event each year of our marriage, I had never participated. To be honest, I felt bad for the little squirrels that I had anthropomorphized in my head, and I would have been scared to shoot one.

Nonetheless, I was always struck by the huge pile of squirrels they collected each year and was more surprised to learn that they weren't just thrown away—all of the meat was donated and happily consumed by the local homeless shelters in the area.

This event, though, was really just an excuse for these sportsmen to spend time in the woods and get tuned up for what everyone was really waiting for a few weeks later: deer season. In the southern United States, deer hunting is religion. As fall comes around each year, southerners talk about two things, college football and deer hunting. Between the weekend football games, most families are out prepping their hunting leases or private land in an effort to attract mythical deer with huge antlers. Depending on the state and regulations, this would include putting out automated corn feeders, planting clover patches, or tending to soybean fields.

After our Arkansas experience, I finally gained the courage to ask my father-in-law if my greenhorn buddy and I could go deer hunting with him. I was expecting him to roll his eyes at the thought of two newbies sitting in his tree stand aiming to take his bucks. But instead he was tickled pink and went into full teacher mode.

Science of Hunting

Over the next few weeks, Alex and I started to receive text messages from my father-in-law that linked to detailed maps of the areas we would be hunting. Those maps were loaded with high-resolution satellite imagery and included dropped pins to where each tree stand was, where every clover patch was laid, and detailed shooting lanes with distance markers. That crash course in deer-hunt planning was bookended by trail photographs of different deer that he had on his properties, along with their usual times of arrival and departure.

This wasn't hunting; this was *science*. We were witnessing the intricacy and seriousness that hunters take in preparation of their craft. This was a full 180-degree turn from what I had come to expect after our hog-hunting experience. I figured we would once again be plopped in the woods, get a slap on the butt, and be told, "Good luck."

In the lead-up to our trip, Alex and I studied those maps like they were going to lead us to *The Lost City of Z*. We talked about where we would sit, how we would communicate, and what it would be like if we harvested a deer. We even called a game processor in the area, in anticipation of a slam-dunk trip to help us turn Bambi into burgers for our families.

With the nip of November in the air, we arrived in Tennessee with our bows in hand for a two-day grind of deer hunting. We showed up like SEAL Team Six, decked out in our new camouflage outfits, our bows in new hard cases, and boots we hadn't yet broken in.

After unpacking, we set out to survey the land that we had been studying on maps for the past few weeks. As we watched the terrain transform from digital pixels (the only way we'd ever seen it before, which was online) into real life features, we both had a swelling of confidence. Hunting is 90 percent preparation, and this was the first time Alex and I were being taught how to prepare in the natural world. It felt amazing.

As we wrapped up our on-foot game planning, we ran into a group of five does, the first herd we would see on that trip, and considered that a good-luck sign for the days to come. With deer tags in our pockets for both does and bucks, and the season officially opening the following day, we headed back to my in-laws' house to get some rest.

First Mishap

The next morning, we were up before four o'clock with Christmas-morning glee as neither of us had been able to sleep through the anticipation. We hurriedly grabbed our prepacked gear and set out in our borrowed Jeep to get to the leased lands trailhead. Once parked, we hopped out into the darkness and turned on our headlamps. Blinding each other in the process, we did a once-over to ensure we both had what we needed:

Bows, check.

Binoculars, check.

Ranger finders, check.

Satisfied that we had not forgotten anything, we took turns doing a "spray down" of each other with over-the-counter, no-scent spray. In hunting, it tends to be a divisive thing where you are either in the camp of using no-scent spray or not. It's kind of like Waffle House versus IHOP.

Either way, Alex and I figured we would use any advantage we could muster and soaked ourselves to the bone. Now that we were dampened, scent-free hunters, we set out down the dark trail to find our tree stands. I walked with Alex to his spot and watched as he shimmied his way safely to the top of his tree. Once he gave me a thumbs up, I turned and set off to find my own spot.

I was surprised at how different the woods, trails, and identifiers looked in the dark. It took me a while, and multiple consultations with my iPhone map, to triangulate where I was in relation to the tree stand I was trying to find. After a few frustrating minutes, I eventually turned on my headlamp to light up the woods around me. Thanks to some reflective tape my father-in-law had put on the tree stand, I was able to quickly find what I was looking for. Without wanting to waste any more time, I got my safety harness on and started to climb the tree.

Once at the top, I settled in for the long sit. It was about forty-five minutes before sunup, and my only job was to be quiet and wait for my quarry to arrive. This seems like an easy task, but in the dark of a predawn morning, you start to tune in to every sound in the woods.

Every tree branch moving and leaf crunching makes you think that the largest deer you could ever imagine is closing in on your location. It was during one of these sober hallucinations, right at first light, that I actually *did* hear a leaf crunch. When I turned in my stand to look at where the sound was coming from, I saw a red light flashing. It took me a few seconds to realize this was Alex approaching on foot, wearing his hunting headlamp. I climbed down the tree with excitement, thinking that he had shot a deer!

The expression on his face carried a different story. In his left hand, he was holding his bow with a limp string completely detached from his cams. For new bowhunters like us, who had no idea how to fix their equipment in the field, this was the kiss of death, and we were less than an hour into our hunt.

As he explained what happened, my heart sank. He'd had his bow hanging beside him on a hook as he sat patiently waiting for sunup. When he went to grab it at the sound of something approaching in the woods, the J-hook caught his string and gently rolled it off his cam without him even noticing it. His bow was now *completely* useless.

With a defeated look, my buddy told me I could stay out, and he would head back to the house to see if he could find a way to get his string back on his bow. However, knowing this would take a specialized tool, a bow press, I decided to head back with him. After a few failed attempts at trying to force the string back on the bow, we turned to Google to see if there were any archery shops in the area. With a stroke of luck, there was one an hour or so drive away that opened at noon. We decided to head out, get his bow fixed, and eat at a Waffle House (now you know where I land on that southern argument). Feeling a little robbed on our forty-eight-hour trip, we licked our wounds over an All-Star Special and started to game plan the next day's adventure.

Killing Field

The next and last morning saw the same ritual de-scenting dance and a dark walk in the woods. The only difference on this day was that we climbed up into the same tree stand, a double-occupancy one, and *carefully* hung our bows on our respective J-hooks. Like the two dorky newbies that we were, we sat and chatted in low voices while our ears picked up every whisper in the forest around us.

Two dorks in a tree.

Shortly after sunup, something happened. We started to hear a distinctively different rustle in the woods surrounding us. One that was different from the birds and squirrels we had been hearing up to that point. It would start and stop in a different pattern. Then, they emerged.

The adrenaline we felt as first-time hunters finally seeing our target game animal was something indescribable and primal. We watched silently as a small herd of does worked their way cautiously out of the tree line and directly into Alex's shooting lane.

With absolutely zero noise, we both instinctively stood up, and my friend grabbed his bow. Every move we made was so calculated and silent that I felt like I was moving through quicksand. We both confirmed the range of the nearest large doe to be thirty yards away, which was pushing the bounds of our comfortable shooting range at the time. With a little encouragement, my friend drew his bow, placed his sight pin on the deer's vital organs, and let an arrow go.

The thwacking sound told us there was an impact, but neither of us knew if the deer was actually hit. As we watched the herd scatter and heard them getting farther and farther away, we did as we were instructed and sat tight.

As a rule of thumb, we wanted to give the injured animal time to expire. If we had made a bad shot, they would likely bed down and pass away, but if we gave chase too quickly, they might spook and try to run, making the recovery process even harder.

After thirty minutes, which felt like hours, we went to inspect the scene. Making our way to the thirty-yard zone, we found my friend's arrow, which had fresh blood from the tip of the broad-head all the way to the end of the nock.

We knew there was a hit.

Caught on trail cam investigating the impact site.

Like Scooby-Doo and his gang, we set out to find blood on any and all surfaces to see which direction his deer had gone. Then with Mr. Magoo–like precision, we got on all fours and tracked drops of blood on fallen leaves, dirt, and tree stumps. After some initial investigating, the trail of blood became more apparent than we had anticipated. Walking slowly in the direction the blood was leading us, we both saw a lifeless form laying on the subtropical Tennessee forest floor, less than sixty yards from where she was first hit.

The prototypical hunter that most people think of would be hooting, hollering, and high-fiving over their beer bellies, but that's not what either of us did. At the moment we found her, there was a palpable and grim sadness to what we had done.

Don't get me wrong. We were both elated that one of us had finally achieved what we had been pursuing for months, and we were proud that our training had paid off. But seeing a beautiful female deer laying there lifeless was more emotional than either of us had anticipated.

We both took a moment and made some soft congratulatory grunts, prayers, and nods to each other, then inspected our harvest. My friend had made a perfect vitals shot that put the deer down quickly and painlessly.

Alex and his first whitetail deer.

We took a few pictures to document the moment. Then, with comic precision we both put our phones away and said, "Shit, now what?"

Our plan all along had been that if either one of us shot a deer that weekend, we would load it into my father-in-law's truck and drive to the processor, a quick thirty minutes away. But what neither of us thought through was that we were in Tennessee, and hunting on an early Sunday morning meant one thing: everything was closed, including our processor.

Standing in the woods, however, and taking in our first intimate experience with an animal's death, we didn't know that yet. So we decided our next step was to get the truck and back it as far into the woods as we could, with the hopes of getting this roughly one-hundred-pound doe loaded into the back.

Alex and I had watched enough hunting videos to know that we needed to field dress that animal, but neither of us knew how. We had been banking on it being the processor's problem. Now it was ours, but we were completely unprepared for it, so we got to work trying to get Bambi's ungutted mom out of the woods.

With some harrowing maneuvers of the borrowed truck, we were able to get it within about eight hundred meters of where next year's meat for our families lay, a distance that seemed reasonably close at the time. For the next hour of the morning, we performed a slapstick reenactment of *Weekend at Bernie's* with our kill. I would grab both hind legs, Alex the front, and we would lift her dead-weight body off the ground and start waddling toward the distant truck. Zapping all of our energy and straining our biceps, we did our best to use our feet to keep her head from banging on every rock we passed.

After shedding layer after layer of clothing in the early morning sun, we found ourselves sweaty, tired, and exhausted. We eventually gave up on our considerate lift-and-waddle method and resorted to disrespectfully dragging her to the bed of the pickup like some mafiosos.

With a final lift to get her into the truck, a feeling of sweet relief washed over us. We shared some high fives, hugs, and excited man-giggles as the shock set in that we had done it.

Our subsequent drive to the processor was amazing. Had our windows been down, we would have been catching bugs in our teeth with the smiles that wouldn't go away. Looking in the rearview mirror, we admired the fur of the beautiful animal we had slain getting matted down by the wind. We both felt like we were in a dream.

As we pulled into the processor's facility, we noticed that there were no cars in the parking lot. Our energy took another sharp turn as we violently returned to earth from our short visit to cloud nine. We got out of our car and started to poke around, until we found a giant cooler out back with a sign that read "Deer Dropoff."

Phew! We were saved.

After another quick round of premature high fives, we started to fill out the paperwork they had lying out back on a blood-stained clipboard. Alex filled in his name, address, pickup date, and license number, but it wasn't until he got to the last line that we noticed the big, bold letters, "PLEASE FIELD DRESS YOUR DEER BEFORE PLACING IN FREEZER." Once again, we began to panic.

Gazing silently, we knew we were hosed. We peeked into the freezer, and sure enough, there was a macabre scene of deer carcasses staring back at us, with perfectly cleaned body cavities. We shut the cooler door, dropped the clipboard, defeatedly hopped back into the car, and discussed what to do next. We figured that our best bet was to head back to our home base and ask my father-in-law to show us what we needed to do for field dressing that deer.

It was vital, however, that we dress the deer in short order, as we could already see the belly beginning to bloat with the rising temperature. Rigor mortis was also setting in, as her legs began to stiffen and point skyward.

I texted my father-in-law, but he was at church. He let me know he could help us in an hour or so when he was home, but the rubber had met the road for my friend and me. It had already been a few hours since our deer was shot, and we couldn't waste any more time. There was no way in our minds that we could dishonor that deer by letting her go to waste, so we quickly drove back to my in-laws' house to dress the deer ourselves using the one true source of knowledge to get us out of that pickle: YouTube. As Alex pulled out his bench-made knife in eager anticipation, I set out to find a step-by-step tutorial.

Off-Field Dressing

Choosing a video arbitrarily, we were now ready for surgery. Like a few underpaid airport baggage handlers, we dropped the deer off the truck bed and onto the pavement. The thwack of her bloated body weight against the cement made us both cringe. Blood from her mouth splattered our dirty camo, a gory foreshadowing of what was to come.

We dragged her a short distance to the grassy yard, which left an unmistakable trail of blood. (Don't ask why we didn't back the truck closer to the grass and unload her there!) With a quick pep talk to each other, we set my iPhone on her hindquarter and prepared to open her chest cavity like seasoned heart surgeons. The video told us to start our knife work at her vent. Not knowing what the vent was, we watched in horror as the grizzled YouTube hunter stuck his knife into his deer's *butthole* and started cutting.

Believing we had stumbled onto a random psychopath's channel, we went to another, and then another, and then another, until we both realized that this was the correct approach. It turns out that cutting around the "vent" loosens the cartilage around the intestinal tract, which needs to pull out cleanly to avoid tainting the meat. So, a few nervous and muffled laughs later, we lifted her beautiful white tail.

Our knifepoint found varying degrees of resistance as we nonartistically began our Civil War–style field surgery. The gummy texture of the anal skin would give way with different pressures, some cuts not going deep enough and others going too deep. With blood now accumulating on my phone screen from hitting stop, rewind, and play, over and over again, we began to make progress. Once the anal cavity was taken care of, we were ready to open her up.

From the genitalia, we made a small incision and began to zip the knife up her belly toward the chest. Our YouTube coach made sure to note that we should be *very* careful here as puncturing the gut bag would release a vomit-inducing stench and further jeopardize the table quality of our meat.

Painstakingly, our knife made its way up to her breastbone. Interestingly, given the bloat that had set in, our deer's intestines forced their way out on their own with every new inch of incision, helping to guide our knife. With the guts now hanging out of our loose-buttholed deer, we went to the next step.

In order to access the vital organs, we needed to punch through a thick membrane wall that separates the heart and lungs from the now protruding intestines, stomach, and gallbladder. With only the breastbone guiding us, we began to cut through the membrane to gain access to the holy grail of meats, the obscure and often tossed-aside organs.

I was thankful this was my friend's deer as I didn't want to be the first one to dive my hands into the crimson soup we were now staring at, which had been slowly warmed by the day's sun. Alex gave a few grunts before diving elbow deep into the cavity. As if looking for a lost set of keys under the couch, he began to swim his hands around. It wasn't long before he asked for my help in identifying what he was blindly touching. Not that I could be of any help in the scientific identification of organs, but I got in there with him anyways.

When my hands first entered the organ cavity, it felt surreal. The acrid smells of the nearby guts burned my nose, and my fingers felt like they were swishing around in a runny tomato bisque. The organs themselves were crammed together and had a rubber-like texture that slipped from my hands as if to avoid being captured.

Performing field surgery for the first time.

We started by pulling out the remnants of the lungs, which were the main ingredient in this lukewarm soup. The pieces of lung were fragile, soft, and seemed to disintegrate between our fingers. Alex's arrow had done quite a beautiful job of deflating the airbags in what is known as a very ethical "double lung" shot.

We then felt around for the heart, the piece of meat we were both excited to eat for both philosophical and health reasons. The iron-rich organ was not hard to find, even though it did not have the cartoonish shape that we often imagine. Instead it resembled an odd-shaped vegetable that we had plucked, just like an apple off a tree.

According to our YouTube shaman, we had but one task left before breaking down the animal for meat, or in our case, taking it to the processor's freezer. We needed to find and cut the esophagus. On our shaman's command, my friend reached even further into the deer, right up to his mid-bicep. The video said to feel for a rubber hose that would lead up toward the deer's mouth. Alex wasn't sure whether he was touching the esophagus or spine, so I was called in to confirm.

Once again putting my full arm into our dead deer, my fingers told me that the spongy nature of what we were touching was definitely not spine and did, in fact, feel like a rubber hose, so we decided to cut it. Blindly, and in an extremely wet cavity, we sliced through what felt like a soaked poblano pepper until we hit bone.

Reverting back to the video, we watched through a red-tinted screen as our instructor seamlessly pulled everything remaining out of the deer by holding on to the cut esophagus and pulling all the way to the vent. Alex squeezed his finger into the garden hose–shaped tube near the throat and began to tug. Although not as pretty as the pros, as we peeled the esophagus back, it magically seemed to detach all of the remaining organs, stomach, and gut bag from the now clean-ish cavity. By the end of the line, all of the internals were barely attached to the deer by the few ligaments we had failed to cleanly cut around the anus in the beginning.

A few snips, and we were free. A beautiful deer full of healthy meat now lay beside us, along with a pile of organs ready to go into the freezer. We were two ecstatic dudes who desperately needed a shot of whiskey at 10:00 a.m. on a Tennessee Sunday.

Relief, pride, and exhaustion washed over us. But our work was not quite over. Though we had finally "field" dressed our deer, it had still been hours since we had shot it, and it needed to be cooled down and laid to rest in the processor's freezer. With the carcass now much lighter and easier to maneuver, we quickly reloaded it into the back of the truck, hosed it down, and cleaned up the pooled blood.

Upon arriving back at the processor, we marked on the form how we wanted the deer to be cut up, placed it in the cooler with a provided unique identifier stapled to its hindquarter, and headed back to my in-laws' house to clean up our mess and dispose of the unusable entrails that remained piled in their yard. Though plenty ignorant, we had done our best to honor the deer's sacrifice for our families. In turn, she had pushed the limits of our comfort and proved that we *could* overcome our fears and do what was needed to survive.

On the way back home to Louisiana, I was able to reflect on how incredible the experience had been. I was no longer just a passive passenger on this earth who expected food to show up on my table, proctored by some technology-based intermediary. I was a part of the land and finally learning the intricacies of harvesting my own protein. Alex and I shared the experience and would share the meat, ultimately growing into better human beings because of it.

Going Solo

Over the next few weekends, I made the long journey back to Tennessee to continue my own pursuit of harvesting my first animal. After a few days on a solo hunt, I was able to harvest my first deer from thirty feet up in a tree, on a Tuesday morning at eight o'clock, one hour before my first work call of the day. The broadhead of my arrow connected with a trotting young buck on the edge of a soybean field with a perfect heart shot, which saw him run just fifty yards before toppling over in peace and sacrifice.

Sitting with my first Whitetail deer in a soybean field.

My solo field-dressing experience was much less dramatic and already felt a bit more routine. It took time, but I followed the same process we had used before and got the same result. The only difference was dealing with male genitalia and feeling sympathy pains in my own "junk" as I cut around the poor buck's family jewels. This morning would also mark the first time in my life that I showed up to a Zoom meeting with blood on my hands, an apropos foreshadowing for the trajectory of my life.

With a true sense of satisfaction with our first big-game hunting season, my buddy and I hung up our bows, cooked some amazing venison tenderloins and deer heart, and started to plan our trip to Tennessee for the next year, thinking this would become an annual adventure.

What neither of us could know then, however, was that this trip would be the last time Alex and I would hunt together. Soon hunting wasn't just going to be a passive hobby for me but an actual way of life.

5

HEADING WEST

My naturally clammy hands became so soaked that I could feel the moisture building up between my knuckles. There was a look in her eyes that I had never seen before—sorrow, relief, and anxiety—the same look I had seen in the eyes of the first deer I had killed just three weeks earlier.

As I rolled my travel suitcase to the side to give my wife a hug, not knowing what story lay behind her emotions, the hair on my neck began to instinctively raise. I could feel that my embrace wasn't being reciprocated, and I felt a growing wet patch on my shoulder. Pulling away, I could see the tears and pained look on her face. With no words said between us, I knew that our journey together was over.

Between her demanding job, her addiction to social media, and our differing views on growing a family, a small rift had opened between us that metastasized over time. Those issues she wrestled with were amplified over the years by my constant traveling and unchecked ambition to always seek more affluence, leading to a slow leak in the foundation of our relationship. Despite the writing on the wall, that night was not something I had expected—perhaps a naive and ego-filled oversight on my part.

We both came from conservative families who preached that you should avoid the "d-word" at all costs. It's probably telling when you put so much emphasis on a word by refusing to even utter it, as if it's Beetlejuice—say it three times and it will appear. But despite the bad juju that our families had associated with the word "divorce," for us, it was coming.

The hollow, confused, and dissociated feeling that consumed me in that moment was a far cry from the primal highs I had felt in Tennessee just a few weeks prior. While on my end-of-year work travels, I had been a broken record, telling anyone that would listen about the benefits and grotesque reality of hunting. I would detail the transformative experience and exclaim that one day I would be a full-time retiree who would hunt all sorts of game whenever I wanted to.

What I didn't know was that the opportunity to grasp my new retirement dream would come sooner than I thought. And when I did grasp it, I wouldn't actually be breaking away completely from my corporate job as I had envisioned. Instead, I'd have to find a way to do my professional work remotely while living a new and challenging life in the backcountry.

As the walls of my well-architected life began to crumble around me, I started reading about the Stoic philosophy called "dichotomy of control." It essentially states that there are certain things we can control and certain things we cannot. I realized that what was happening to my marriage, to the comfortable life we had built, and the effect of us telling our families about our plans to divorce were out of my control. What remained in my control was where I went from that point in time, which scared the shit out of me.

Sealing My Fate

With nowhere to hide, cry, or think deeply, I decided to get away. With little fanfare, planning, or expectations, I packed a few personal belongings: the frozen deer meat I had just received back from the Tennessee processor; my hunting gear and clothes; and my laptop, which I'd need to work remotely in an arrangement I'd negotiated with my tech employer. Within a week, I was road-tripping across the Western United States to Idaho.

Why Idaho?

The year prior, my now soon-to-be-ex-wife and I had gone through our usual decision tree of figuring out where to take our yearly vacation. After listing all of the typical tropical destinations, I threw out an idea that we should go somewhere different. I suggested somewhere in our own backyard, stateside, that offered up mountains and lakes instead of sand and cocktails.

Putting a finger on the map, we landed on giving Idaho a shot. We flew to Boise, the capital city, then traveled to the now well-known town of Stanley on the north side of the Sawtooth Wilderness to hike and explore. Ultimately, it was this chance trip that would seal my fate and tie me to that state forever.

Within an hour of landing and starting our drive north to the mountains, we saw elk, mule deer, wild turkeys, antelope, and bald eagles, leaving me gobsmacked and curious as to how I had been clueless that this all existed in this oft-forgotten state.

After an amazing week of exploring, our trip ended with an experience I will never forget. While blindly searching for an alpine lake, we found ourselves on a snow-covered trail that was hard to navigate without snowshoes. A few slow steps into the trail, we both stopped to look at each other with a nervous glance and simultaneously mentioned that we felt we were being followed.

We stopped to look around, and on a steep ridgeline to our right, we caught a quick glimpse of something moving. Holding our breath, which was in short supply due to the altitude, we watched as a magnificent light-gray wolf stepped out from between the pines—my spirit animal.

I felt my wife grab my arm as a primal fear took hold of both of us. At that moment, I was glad that my wife had been able to carry her Federal service pistol on our flight, even though she was looking to me for comfort at that moment. With our eyes locked on this animal, I fumbled for my phone to try to snap a picture. In the time it took for me to pull out my phone and open my camera, the wolf was gone. It disappeared so quickly and silently that we both questioned whether we had really just seen it. The only confirming sign that we weren't delusional was the adrenaline that was coursing through our bodies.

In that fleeting moment, I told my wife that we were moving there. I wasn't sure when or how, but I felt a calling to those woods, and I would not deny listening to my soul. I had no idea then that it would be just a few months later that I'd find myself mourning for what I'd lost, but with my finger back on the map of Idaho, and my car pointed due north. As I pulled out of our driveway on a warm January morning, I wasn't sure if I would ever return to that beautiful home in south Louisiana that we had spent years building together.

Go West, Young Man

On my way to Idaho, I only stopped twice. Once, at a small hotel in the high desert of New Mexico to get some rest and catch up on work emails, and again at Arches National Park in Utah. When I rolled into the national park, it was predawn, and patches of snow littered the red rocks all around me. In an effort to lift my spirits and experience something new, I decided to see the famed Delicate Arch, the largest in the park, which I'd viewed many times with my wife on Instagram as one influencer or another struck an exaggerated pose underneath it.

When I drove up to the trailhead parking lot, I was greeted by a sign stating that the roughly two-mile trail to the arch was closed due to dangerous ice conditions. Sitting alone in my car, fighting back sobs as old memories randomly flooded my brain, I decided to ignore the signage and go anyway. I pulled out a pair of running shorts and shoes from one of my bags, and deck changed in the driver's seat of my car. I stepped out into the cold and set off on a jog toward the arch.

I encountered a couple on the trail who were equally ignorant to the warnings that had been posted at the trailhead. With some polite pleasantries, I passed them and kept moving. The trail was fine, and I made great time until I got to within four hundred meters of the arch. This last stretch was up a steep single-track trail that was completely blocked from the sun by a sheer rock face. It was not a technical climb, but I found out quickly why the trail was closed. That short portion of trail was completely covered in black ice. To make things sketchier, the drop-off to my left was severe and unforgiving.

As I began to climb, I found my body naturally sinking closer and closer to Earth to try and grip as much surface area as possible. Eventually I was crawling on all fours as I slowly moved toward the top. Ahead, I could see the morning sunlight hitting the trail where the ice ended, and I kept on crawling. At one point, the water bottle I had been carrying in my left hand slipped away and followed the iceluge back down the trail, before careening off into the abyss with an audible smack on the valley floor a few seconds later.

Feeling bad for accidentally littering in the park, I considered, briefly, trying to climb down and get it before thinking better of the idea. After thirty minutes of slow crawling, I made it to the sunlight and was able to quickly regain traction under my shoes. It was just a short push to the top where I crested over to see the famed arch.

My timing was perfect for a beautiful sunrise, and I had the entire area to myself. Sitting there and taking in the scenery, I began to think about everything that had transpired in the last few months of my life and what my future held. I sat and prayed for an answer to the many questions in my head about what it meant to be happy.

As I prayed, a crow landed nearby and worked its way to within just a few feet of me. Though often seen as a bad omen, I found a lot of peace sitting and staring at that bird. I had never been that close to one before, and the deep colors of its feathers reflecting the morning sun emitted an almost iridescent glow. As we stared at each other, I could feel the crow's mental cognition as it tried to read me.

The Hopi and Navajo people are indigenous to those lands, and their ancient petroglyph drawings can still be seen on some of the red rocks. They consider seeing a single black crow as a sign of change usually brought about by death. Thankfully for me, death for the Hopi and Navajo nations was not necessarily tied to the physical realm but to the spiritual body as well.

The crow and me at Arches National Park.

That crow and I sat together for what felt like ten minutes, before it finally gave me a jolting squawk and flapped off. As I heard the air displace under its wings with a louder-than-expected whooshing sound, I knew in my heart that I would never go back to Louisiana or to my wife.

In that moment, taking in the beautiful sunrise, I knew that my journey back to happiness lay out in wild places—out in the mountains where Mother Gue in the film *Jeremiah Johnson* felt that only "the animals and savages" go—a place where I would leave behind the negative elements of technology. My former spiritual self was dead. I left the old me right there in that natural bowl, below that famous arch, and silently said a prayer as I slowly spread the invisible remnants of my figurative ashes.

With my mental shackles loosened, I left the arch, slid back down the trail, and made it back to my car to resume my drive north. Hours later, when I rolled into the clean and growing metropolis of Boise, I found a place to crash—a month-to-month apartment that would serve as a launching point to explore the Gem State and to find a more permanent place to hang my hat. For the next few weeks, I put my corporate aspirations on hold by taking a short-term leave and went about finding the perfect place to grieve, learn, and ultimately build a new way of life.

Exploring the whole state of Idaho was eye-opening for me. There was no state more beautiful and filled with wonder: desert moonscapes, twelve-thousand-foot peaks, hot springs, clear rivers, and every game animal you could imagine.

It was a paradise.

I looked at properties and dilapidated cabins in the Lemhi Valley where Lewis and Clark first unfurled the American flag west of the rockies, the Frank Church Wilderness of No Return where beavers were once parachuted in to repopulate and de-timber the area, and up to the clearwater region where the Nez Pearce people once freely roamed the landscape.

All of those places were beautiful, stunning actually, but one place deep in the Sawtooth Wilderness captured my heart and mind. It was a small town at the base of a ten-thousand-foot granite-faced mountain, at the end of a seventy-mile dirt road. To get there, I had to follow precarious cliffs and switchbacks as the road climbed to over six thousand feet, with no signs of civilization and no cell phone service.

Along the primitive road, restorative hot springs crept out of the river in imprecise intervals, reminding any intrepid passerby that this Eden sat atop the world's largest supervolcano, Yellowstone, and could shake them off like a flea if it ever wanted to. That magnitude of raw power in a landscape was like nothing I had ever experienced. Only thirty-something intrepid souls toughed it out in the small town year round.

I was sold.

With a lot of luck, my arrival in Idaho happened to coincide with one of the few available properties in town popping up for sale, and I pounced on the opportunity. As if by divine intervention, the second that I made those final pen strokes to close on my tiny cabin, the world also made its pen stroke on nationwide COVID lockdowns.

As I prepared to leave the safety of a metropolitan city for the backcountry, I saw before my eyes shops closing, toilet paper disappearing from shelves, and people acting irrationally at the supply chain breakdown. Meat aisles at grocery stores were empty, and people were coming to blows over bottles of water in department store parking lots. Chaos and a sense of helplessness were blanketing the country, and I, too, felt the fear.

As someone who had just harvested and gutted an animal for the first time just months before, I was still green behind the ears. Yet, with a cooler full of frozen deer meat to keep me fed for the next few months, I had a tiny shred of confidence that I could now survive if everything stayed shut down for an extended period.

I knew I was about to learn to chop the wood that would warm my house, kill the animals that would fill my belly, use their skins to put clothes on my back, and slowly release the noose of dependency that was attached to a large and now failing machine. This brought me peace.

With that naive optimism, I pulled out of Boise one last time and made the solo trip deep into the backcountry, into a land where every action would finally carry a true consequence. One that would be much different than expected, and one that would teach and humble me in ways I could not imagine.

Spirit Animal Redux

As my tires released their traction from the paved road, I saw the sign cautioning me of the primitive road I would be taking for the next seventy miles. I smiled. As that smile crept across my face, a light-colored wolf stepped into view on the wood line—just as one had done several months before, when I made the verbal commitment to one day return and live in the Sawtooths.

Sign on the way to my cabin.

Staring at a distance into this beautiful animal's eyes, I could feel a tectonic shift in my core. I was no longer the human I had been for the past thirty-one years. I was something new. I didn't know what that was yet, but I was committed to blindly following the spiritual pull of this land.

Yet as quickly as that moment came, it was gone. The wolf turned and disappeared into the timber, and I once again felt small. My tucked-away fears and insecurities rushed into the forefront of my mind in the shape of doubt, and I wrestled with them for the rest of the drive to my new homestead.

Humble Pie

Hours later, when I pulled into town, there was no ticker-tape parade for this outsider. As I would later appreciate, new folks rolling into town are met with skepticism and general disdain. Not because the community is filled with mean people, but there was an ethos and a way of life out there that people expected you to uphold. Simply saying that you are "self-sufficient" wasn't good enough. You needed to prove it.

And prove it I did not—at least not initially.

In fact, the first few nights in my cabin saw me nearly freeze to death, as I could not figure out how to maintain a warm fire in my own home. The accumulating lack of sleep over a few nights started affecting my performance at my remote tech job. This exhaustion, coupled with intermittent internet outages, was starting to affect my mental resolve, until I eventually summoned the humility to tuck my tail and ask my nearest neighbor a half mile away to show me how to light and maintain my wood-burning stoves. With some eyebrow-raised chuckles, my jovial neighbor explained the mechanics and chemistry of burning wood for home heating.

As it turns out, fire needs oxygen (duh), and the flue, the thing that controls oxygen flow, on my stoves had been shut. This was making my attempts at a warm fire impossible. I felt stupid and embarrassed, feelings I would be getting more and more comfortable with as I fumbled my way through this new and harsh way of life.

With the new ability to warm my cabin and sleep soundly through the night, I started to build out a wishlist of animals I wanted to have interactions with over the coming years through hunting and trapping. Each evening, after my house chores and remote work were done, I would do research on hunting. My research was focused on which licenses and tags I would need to secure in order to pursue the big-game animals that first attracted me to these lands. Each night, I went to bed with optimistic visions of future success.

I imagined touching the antlers of my first downed elk, the yet-un-known taste of antelope carnitas, and pulling on my first pair of beaver-lined mittens. For all of my negative qualities, blind ambition was one thing that I certainly had enough of to spare.

Reality, however, is often different than what you imagine it to be. In my case, unbeknownst to me, my images of what success looked like were about to get pimp-slapped by Mother Nature. I was about to swallow pill after pill of reality checks, and be force fed humble pie until I puked.

Though I knew in my heart that my optimism wasn't seated in reality, I was excited, I had a plan, and it was time to execute.

PART II

ART OF THE ARCHER

We must learn to reawaken and keep ourselves awake, not by mechanical aid, but by an infinite expectation of the dawn.

—HENRY DAVID THOREAU

6

ELK

I could hear the rocks making an impact in the dry gully, hundreds of yards below me. In the pitch-black predawn, I could vaguely make out small sparks being set off by the shod hooves of the horse in front of me, my only indication that I was still on the trail.

I was scared.

As I felt the unsure steps of the horse I was on, my thighs instinctively tightened to the saddle leather, and my double-hand grip squeezed the horn until my knuckles were white. I had not been on a horse since I was eight years old, yet here I was working my way up to a nine-thousand-foot peak in the darkness of an early September morning, wearing a thirty-pound pack with my bow dangling from the back.

I was less than thirty minutes into my first Idaho archery elk hunt, way out of my comfort zone, and questioning the last few months of preparation I had undergone at my remote cabin. This was going to be one hell of a grocery store run.

The day before, I had awakened in my cabin at 3:00 a.m. in excited anticipation. I'd thrown my prepacked duffle bags, bows, and other assorted gear into my truck, and started the sojourn to the beautiful town of Stanley, the place where I first fell in love with Idaho. I made great time on the long dirt road out of my new town, slowed only by one stubborn porcupine, and I was able to sync up with the owner of Mystic Saddle Outfitters by 10:00 a.m., just as I had planned.

As part of the master plan I had been conjuring up in the loneliness of my new mountain cabin, I had decided that to overcome my uncountable hunting deficiencies, I would need help. So, for my first backcountry elk hunt, I would be working with a guide.

Not only would this keep me from dying, but my hypothesis was that if I could go with a seasoned elk guide, I would pick up more knowledge in one trip than I could in five years of do-it-yourself hunting. I considered it an investment in myself and a potential shortcut to beating down the tough learning curve I was about to go through.

After quickly signing a liability waiver, I followed one of the ranch hands down a long, windy road that led to the trailhead we would be departing from, deep in Idaho's White Clouds Wilderness.

While waiting at the trailhead with the crew that would make this whole guided experience a reality, I got to meet the workhorses that would haul us up and down precarious trails for the next eight days to areas over ten thousand feet. My noble steed was a gassy, grumpy, and hungry horse named Hollister.

My horse, Hollister, and me at ten thousand feet.

After an all-too-short introduction to the basics of how to make the horse go, stop, and veer left and right, I very ungracefully mounted Hollister, and we were underway.

Base Camp

The three and a half hours that it took us to get from the trailhead to base camp were equal parts mesmerizing and painful. As we slowly passed patches of aspens, I couldn't help but have mental wanderlust for what the week ahead would hold. Meanwhile,

I was feeling a growing pain in my backside as I tried in vain to figure out how to properly sit in the saddle.

At about two in the afternoon on day one, we trotted into our base camp. Having never been on a guided hunt, I had zero clue as to what I should expect from an outfitter. I wasn't even sure I would be fed. I was just crossing my fingers that I could ration the twelve Clif Bars that were stuffed in my pack for the whole week, if need be. But riding into camp set all of those minor worries aside, as I saw the legitimacy of the operation.

Camp for the week.

One other hunter and I shared our own canvas wall tent, which was flanked by another tent for our two guides. There was also a large mess tent where our Mormon ranch hand and cook resided.

In pretty short order, we dropped our gear, changed, and were off to see if we could locate any elk out of the gate. For this first evening's hunt, we went off as a group of four on foot to do some scenario practice and elk calling.

I'm not sure if it was the altitude, the long day, or just my inherent weakness, but within a few hundred yards, I was breathing like a fat kid playing dodgeball. It was at that exact moment that I thought, *I'll have to really suck it up if I want to make it through this and be an effective shot when the opportunity presents itself.*

All of the training, all of the cool high-speed gear, and all of the podcasts and articles I'd read didn't prepare me for what it really felt like to hunt at elevation in the Rockies. Regardless, once I was able to get my heart rate back to baseline, we let out our first elk calls and waited. Lucky for us, we were hunting during the peak rutting time, which is when male elk are looking to procreate and are super horny. Those rutting bulls are very vocal and will respond to other male calls, known as bugles, and come in to run off the potential intruder.

The anticipation I felt waiting to hear my first elk bugle response was tension filled. I started to count, and I made it all the way to "three Mississippi" when I heard that beautiful, deep, guttural sound echo out of the pines below us. I was so ecstatic and high on euphoria that I didn't even notice our guides laughing and turning around.

Wait, what happened? Why aren't we chasing after that elk?

Well, it turned out that my very first "authentic" Idaho elk bugle was just other hunters across the ridge trying the same noble pursuit. This would be harder than I thought.

Knowing that the area was now busted, we hiked our way back to camp where we were greeted with a hot meal of beef tenderloin and beer and had some time to unwind before hitting the sack.

Shut Up and Get Down

On the first real morning of our hunt, I was awakened by the sound of our wall tent unzipping. That stirred me awake in a panic as my fight-or-flight instincts kicked in. I was ready to choke out whatever came through the fabric door. But that adrenaline dump quickly extinguished as one of our jovial guides came in to greet my tent mate and me with a hot cup of coffee.

With my bowel-moving brew in hand, I fumbled to get my gear ready for the day and met everyone at the mess tent. Our camp cook was busy whipping up some good eats as my neurons fired images of bugling bulls into my mind's eye at an unnerving rate.

After a full meal and a quick run to the nearest hole in the ground, we were ready to roll out. My guide and I saddled up and took off in a direction that led us up some steep embankments and rocky hills, where my horse seemed less sure-footed than I cared for. I was just glad we were doing this in the dark because the trails were washed out and sketchy. I preferred not to see.

After a forty-five-minute ride through dark timber, where I managed to snag my bow on every tree limb, we broke through to see daylight, tied the horses, and set out on foot.

Within thirty yards of the horses, in a little outcropping, my guide gave me the universal sign language for "shut up and get down," which I promptly adhered to. I followed his gaze toward the adjacent ridge. With a child-like glee, I saw three bulls trailing each other like some sort of conga line. With some quick instruction from my guide, I set out for a tree about one hundred yards in front of him while he started his elk calling regimen: bugle, cow call, cow call, bugle, elk chuckle. It went like this for a good thirty minutes, with only a minimal head-tilting reaction from those bulls. To my dismay, they slowly meandered over the far ridge line.

Calling for elk in the early morning light.

We set out in hot pursuit, but our chase was ultimately not successful. This was the story of the day as we put in close to eight boot miles in high elevation, with no luck getting answers to any of our calls or seeing any more animals.

We eventually turned it in and were back in camp around seven that evening, where we followed the same drill as the night before: delicious food (spaghetti, if memory serves), beer, recollections of our follies in the woods, and some of the best stories that no ears beyond those tents would ever get the joy of hearing.

Scent on the Wind

On the second morning, we followed the same pattern: coffee, eat, shit, and saddle up. That would be the regimen every morning, but each day I was a little stiffer and ever more sore. So I increased my ibuprofen consumption, something I had only previously done to stave off the regular migraines I would get staring at a computer screen for hours on end.

We set out for the same area where we had limited luck the day before. Despite my best intentions for success, we ran into a new and pervasive issue: the wind.

No matter where we went, the wind was ripping. On the tops of ridges, it had to be gusting in excess of fifty miles per hour, and none of our elk calls came back answered. Despite the frustration, my guide was teaching me as much about backcountry hunting as he possibly could. We hunkered in timber to avoid the onslaught of wind and talked about tracking, calling, elk signs, and predator issues.

Around midday, I saw my guide perk up. His nostrils flared like a bloodhound on the scent of an escaped convict. He whispered that there had to be an elk within fifty yards of where we sat because he could smell it so strongly. He was so confident that he had me nock an arrow just to be sure. After some silent coaching, I was able to catch the sharpie-under-the-nose whiff of what was undeniably a large elk nearby.

Despite the brief excitement, the scent slowly faded away, along with our hopes of getting into a rutting bull. More boot miles, more tracking lessons, and we eventually called it a day as the sun began to set.

Days in the Pines

With the days ticking away, our guides decided to take a different approach. We set out for a new area with steeper terrain and denser pine forest to explore.

From the jump, we started getting answers to our bugles, which was exhilarating but led to yet another recurring theme: quick descents down steep mountains and slow, agonizing climbs on foot back from the depths of hell.

It's hard to articulate with words just how difficult it is to get near enough to a herd of elk, hear their calls, analyze the terrain, and make decisions quick enough for a chance to shoot a bull or cow with archery equipment.

Yet multiple times over the next several days on those slopes, we were able to close in on a herd. We were within forty yards of huge bulls sending bone-rattling bugles toward us.

Despite our best efforts, however, every time we closed the distance, dust devils of swirling wind wrecked our chances.

It was insane and awe-inspiring how these huge animals could be so vocal, so horned-up and ready to fight or screw, and then go absolutely silent within a matter of seconds as the wind switched direction.

Wind be damned, we would traverse up and down what my guide and I started to call "Shit Sandwich Mountain." Like a scene from the movie *Dumb and Dumber,* we would find ourselves snapping out of our adrenaline-filled elk chase and realize that yet again, we were at the bottom of that cursed mountain. Each time, we had to climb back to the top to chase more elk.

Sitting atop "Shit Sandwich Mountain."

As an old wrestling coach used to tell me, "If you're going to eat a shit sandwich, you don't nibble." So like good soldiers, we would shut up and make our way back to the top to put in more work.

Feeling tired and defeated after doing the shit sandwich dance four and a half times in less than six hours, we started to make our way back to the horses. My guide made some half-hearted bugles as we neared. Lo and behold, we got some responses. Without thinking of the pain we had already been through, we scrambled down a ridge to get in position one more time.

This was it.

We had two large bulls actively responding to our calls, and we could hear them closing the distance with the wind working in our favor for the first time that week. I took my time and got set up where I thought the bulls would come through. I had a clear shooting lane to my right and a marginally clear lane to my left. I set about finding the distance to nearby trees with my laser rangefinder and started going through my mental checklist to prepare for a shot.

I was going through my list for a third time when it happened. For the first time in my life, I saw huge, beautiful elk horns making their way gracefully through the timber heading in my direction. It was a shock to the system to see how majestic these animals really were. It sent a shot of adrenaline so deep into my soul that I lost sight of the fact that this was a moment a few years in the making.

Once I saw the bull elk's face, I instinctively drew my bow. But the elk was taking his time, and I'd need to wait until he was closer. After a few seconds, I had to let my bow down in order for the big bull to meander into a clearer and closer shooting lane.

In that lull, I was able to re-range the clearing that I expected him to walk through, approximately thirty-five yards away. With a quick adjustment to my sight, I redrew my bow and put my center sight pin, the equivalent of a rifle scope's crosshairs, on that area until his vitals were in view. The moment I'd waited so long for was finally here. I punched the trigger on my bow release, heard the air displaced from my arrow leaving the string, and watched in dismay as my arrow burrowed into the dirt at the elk's feet.

By some divine intervention, that beauty of a bull elk ignored my errant arrow and remained focused on the cow call my guide was making one hundred yards behind me. I raced to put a new arrow on my string and quickly re-ranged my bull, which now showed him to be at forty-seven yards. I must have accidentally picked up a limb or some other closer debris on my first attempt to gauge the proper distance to the animal, which led to a terrible miscalculation. No matter. I adjusted my sight and once again redrew my bow. I put my pin on his vitals for a second time and sent my arrow downrange.

In silent horror I watched as my second arrow sailed two inches above the elk's back, which the bull sensed immediately. With cat-like reflexes, this one-thousand-pound beast pivoted on a dime and ran off into the fading light of our sixth and most exciting day of hunting.

I knew immediately that I had not hit the bull, but in an abundance of caution, we spent the next hour trying to find my arrows to see if we could detect any blood. We gave up after darkness set in and went back to camp to follow the same end-of-day routine. This time, however, the food seemed a bit blander, the beer a bit staler, the stories less enthralling, and my sleep a lot less sound. I felt close to frustrated tears with my disappointment, questioning my preparation for the hunt and constantly replaying the event in my head. But with two days of hunting left, I tried to put those thoughts out of my mind.

Unknowingly about to miss my first elk.

A Day of Silence

Our first order of business the next day was to go back to the scene of the crime to ensure that I hadn't wounded that bull elk, despite my insistence that I really had fumbled two shots. It took several hours, after which we set out in pursuit of more elk.

But Mother Nature had different plans and decided to send us heavy snow, which silenced every bull for miles. That silence was the perfect environment to stew on the fatal errors I had made the day before. I was dealing with the difficult range of emotions a hunter must go through when they miss a golden opportunity to provide their own food source. That cold, mentally exhausting, and bugle-less day had me thinking about my journey to that point. I had so much more to learn about hunting and self-sufficiency to even get to an elementary baseline.

Back at camp that evening, the crew fed us a hot meal of pulled pork sandwiches, and we all quietly turned in before the last full day of hunting.

The familiar cadence of coffee, eat, shit, and saddle up kicked off the final day, with determination and blind faith as my only drivers. It was my last chance to bag an elk, and my guide and I were willing to go to the ends of the earth to make something happen.

We decided to go back to the same area where we had seen elk on days four and five. With *Groundhog Day* precision, we once again found ourselves chasing the same herd of bulls through the same timber, busted by wind once again at the bottom of Shit Sandwich Mountain.

Knowing it was our last day, we traversed back to the top with bigger smiles and more painful steps. Yes, our prospects were fading, and I had already failed, but a sense of gratitude permeated our efforts. Despite the pain and frustration, I was learning, and I was in love with the natural environment. We did that same act several more times throughout the day but could never quite get the bulls to commit. As the day wound down, and the realization set in that my first backcountry elk hunt was coming to a close without harvesting an animal, I had one pervasive emotion: gratitude.

Yes, I was mad at myself for missing the one opportunity that had presented itself. But after some reflection, I was proud of my preparation. I was leaving everything on the mountain, and with the help of my guide, I'd had experiences that accelerated my elk-hunting knowledge in ways I could have never achieved on my own.

As a consolation prize, I was able to shoot my first grouse on the way back to camp, which made for a great snack. It gave me an ironic giggle as I realized I was able to hit a small bird out of a tree at thirty yards with my bow, yet I'd missed a one-thousand pound giant at forty-seven yards. Go figure.

Pulling out the grouse beast.

Within a few hours of returning to camp, we were back on the horses and heading back to the trailhead singing old country tunes. It felt not much different than what folks like Jeremiah

Johnson and Del Gue may have done in similar mountains, over one hundred and fifty years ago.

As I said goodbye to the crew, I was feeling optimistic, but the drive home was more difficult than I had anticipated. I drove in silence for five hours, replaying the events that had led up to my missed shots, mental torture that would stick with me for the next year. When I got home to my cabin that evening, I had one final act of humility to go through, which was to unload the bags of ice from the empty Yeti coolers I had purchased for my game meat.

The disappointment of my mistakes would ease over the coming months and only occasionally boil to the surface when friends or extended family would ask me about my trip. With the benefit of hindsight and time, I realized that the experience had been the perfect baptism for me. The open space, fresh air, and physical exertion were the therapeutic tonic that I had needed. And as the elk season closed, mule deer season was just kicking off. I would have the opportunity to apply my learnings to my next woodland pursuit and get more chair time with the ultimate therapist: the hunt.

7

MULE DEER

The late August sun was just cresting the ten-thousand-foot peak above me. Feeling its first rays on the back of my neck was a welcome gratification, as I had been shivering on that hillside since 4:00 a.m. I was slowly crawling up a small bluff covered in sagebrush, light snow, and burnt timber—a natural obstacle course that made it extremely difficult to be stealthy.

Inch by inch, I worked my way forward, slithering over logs, awkwardly holding my bow, while coaching myself on how these deliberate and slow movements would pay off. Every cold and painful move was calculated. I was making sure that I stayed upwind of my target and was playing the thermal drafts perfectly. I was putting to use all of the hard-earned learnings I had collected over the last two years living and hunting in the backcountry.

Aside from my growing skills as an archer and woodsman, I had also been blessed to meet and build a relationship with an Idaho native, Olesya, in that same time period of accelerated learning. A true mountain woman, she was drawn to my new way of life, which balanced a high-tech career and rugged outdoorsmanship. The wilderness was something she had cared for deeply her entire life, camping with her family as a child and eventually spending months of her life living out of a tent, exploring trails all around the Pacific Northwest as a young adult. Our connection was instantaneous, pure, and intoxicating. Within a short period, we were married. She moved into my cabin with me, helped start our gardening efforts, and made my life markedly less lonely. In short order, we were expecting our first child. As such, the success of this particular morning's hunt for mule deer held much more weight, as my new and growing family desperately needed the meat to help fill our near-empty freezers.

Solo Backcountry Hunt

The days leading up to that hillside stalk had seen the familiar kaleidoscope of emotions that I had now become accustomed to on a solo backcountry hunt: elevation gain, exhaustion, thirst, stunning views, self-doubt, frustration, boredom, elation, adrenaline, and depression—the full, albeit manic, human experience.

Just twelve hours prior, I had successfully flushed three mule deer out of a web of seven-feet-tall chaparral bushes. Neither they nor I had expected the late evening run-in, and when they caught my scent, they hightailed it to the next ridge.

Fortunately, they never actually saw me. That had given me an opportunity to effectively use my laser range finder to approximate the distance to the lead doe and prepare myself for a shot. At seventy-three yards, it would be a test of my growing abilities as an archer and push the bounds of an ethical shot. After some mental judo, I convinced myself that the thousands of arrows I had shot at that distance or greater had prepared me for that moment. So with self-persuasion measured in milliseconds, I'd started my familiar shot protocol.

Once I'd found my familiar anchor points and had the stationary doe in my front sight, I pulled my scapula together to engage my back-tension release and let an arrow fly. In anticipation of a hit, I looked up from my bow only to see the three deer slowly walk away as if nothing had happened.

Confused, tired, and immediately disappointed, I walked over to investigate the scene. With no blood, no sign of my arrow, and a setting sun, I was forced into making quick decisions. I could have followed the deer and risked spooking them, or just left the site to sneak back at first light to find them in their now-known bedding area. Choosing the latter is how I ended up on that hillside again, belly down now, and freezing my ass off trying to execute a perfect stalk at daybreak.

After almost an hour of crawling, I found myself within fifty yards of where I had last seen the three deer and had taken the failed shot the evening before. Taking another slow lurch forward, I heard the unmistakable sound of dried sagebrush crunching less than thirty yards in front of me.

The cortisol in my body spiked, and I could intuit that there was a deer within a very short distance from where I lay. That chemical dump allowed my entire body to freeze and focus on slow and deliberate movements. I periscoped my neck slowly over the fallen timber in front of me to see if I could get eyes on my prey.

As I peered over a soot-covered stump, it took my mind a few seconds to catch up to what my body was immediately telling me: fight or flight! A large American black bear was grunting and pawing the ground a mere stone's throw away.

The black bear who took my kill.

Dipping down in haste, with the sudden gut-wrenching awareness that my pistol was safely stowed back at camp a few miles away, I immediately put an arrow on my bow as a self-defense measure. Mustering what courage I could, I peered back over the log to see what my fate may be.

The skills I had picked up on my first guided hunt were continuing to pay off. My proper playing of the wind was masking my scent from the bear. In fact, it started to trot its way further downwind from me at an astonishing clip, allowing me to sit up and watch it work gracefully through the rugged terrain. I was in awe, finally able to relax, take a few pictures, and make some strategic realizations.

First, with a bear in the area, the likelihood of my deer still being around was almost nil, and I knew my hunt was a bust. Second, as I watched the bear, it dawned on me that it was taking the exact path the previously assumed unharmed deer had taken the evening before.

As I sat there feeling sorry for myself over my wasted efforts, I decided to follow the bear to see what had drawn its attention. When I got to the fallen tree where the lead doe had been standing the evening before, I saw what I'd missed the first time: my spent arrow lying on the ground.

I was hesitant to pick it up because I didn't want the grief of seeing blood on that arrow, which would have meant that I'd actually made a hit the evening before. It took just a slight bend at my hips for my eye to see the perfect heart blood painted from the tip of my arrow's broadhead, down the shaft, and all the way to the fletchings and nock. A rush of guilt, more confusion, and mental playbacks were firing in my head at rates I couldn't comprehend.

How was there blood on my arrow if I'd missed the deer? If I didn't miss the deer, then how did it just walk off? Had I missed my opportunity to fill our freezer with meat *again* this season? How will I tell this to my wife and friends? And where is my deer?

At some point in my internal interrogation, enough of my brain cells joined together to connect me to the fact that the bear I was following had been tracking my deer. With a bit of adrenaline-fueled machismo emanating from my core, I took off toward the edge of the bluff to see what lay on the other side.

Within just a few steps, I was able to peer fifty feet below me to see not one but *two* bears eating the deer that I had unknowingly taken with a perfect seventy-three-yard heart shot the night before. With plenty of daylight left, I sat down and watched this macabre show for hours. I played back the mistakes on repeat until I felt physically ill. Finally, I convinced myself to be thankful that this animal had not gone to waste and was ultimately being consumed by other animals in the food chain.

My internal pep talk helped, but I had failed again. It was an unsettling and recurring theme in my learning to be a self-sustained woodsman. I now had to go home and tell Olesya, who was with our five-month-old daughter, that we would once again be meatless for the foreseeable future. It was a confession that impacted me more than her, but one that I still dreaded.

I'd filled my tag, which means I'd killed a deer and my hunting season was over, but I'd been cheated out of the meat by two hungry black bears.

Though my second season's journey came to an end that day, there were still opportunities to help my friends try to fill their freezers, and to apply the hard lessons I had learned. Such acts of knowledge sharing made us all sharper and better hunters.

Mountain Hunt

Two days later, my friend Kyle was up at our cabin. We were planning to hike eight miles into the backcountry, gain over three thousand feet in elevation, and cross over a steep mountain range to get into the hunting unit that he had a deer tag for.

Having prepped with the aid of our online mapping service, we set out with our tent, meals, and equipment early on a Saturday morning, expecting a difficult day's journey. We spent the morning in the low valleys, slowly working our way up in elevation. We stopped to eat lunch and enjoy the scenery before embarking on what would be one of the most intense days of hiking that either of us had ever experienced.

After a few hours on still-stable legs, we eventually reached the crossing point that we had marked on the map. It was a steep ascent that was riddled with fallen and burned timber from a fire the previous year. As we had been able to tell from the online map, this was the best place to cross over into the hunting unit. In fact, it was our best option out of many more perilous and rock-faced options.

Peering up that mountain with heavy packs on our backs, we thought twice as we chugged water from a stream at its base. It was hot and only going to get hotter, so we wanted to make sure we were well hydrated. Our mapping service indicated a natural spring at the top of the mountain, but we still filled our water bottles for the next few hours climbing.

While cooling off in the shade, we began glassing the hillside we were about to embark upon. We sighted a herd of deer near the top, which gave us the necessary energy to bite the proverbial bullet and get to hiking.

It is incredibly hard to articulate what it feels like to cover two thousand feet of elevation in just three-quarters of a mile. Slogging over dead timber, slipping on rock scree, and silently suffering, we would stop every fifty or so yards to pick out our next waypoint—a tree, a bush, or anything—to focus on for short bursts of steep and heavy hiking.

Word of advice: pick short hunting partners.

Keeping up with my tall and gangly legged hiking partner meant that I needed to take two steps for every one of his, which was physically and mentally taxing. So much so, that if I could give one piece of advice for new backcountry hunters, it would be to choose partners that are shorter than you. Nonetheless, over the next few hours, we sweated and incrementally made our way to the top of the mountain, which bordered the hunting unit we were targeting, and set up our camp.

Unloading heavy tent and camp equipment from our rucksacks after that arduous hike was nothing short of glorious. After eight miles of hiking and two thousand feet of gain, our muscles were screaming, so we chugged the bulk of our water to stave off dehydration on the abnormally hot day.

Once unpacked, tent pitched, we took our day packs and bows to make the final push to the summit to glass into the next basin. On the way up, we would be passing by the natural spring we marked on the map to refill our water for the next day and a half of hard hunting.

High altitude mule deer campsite.

As we pushed up the last few hundred meters, we were happy. Our packs were lighter, our legs more springy, and we would be getting into virgin hard-to-reach territory soon—we could see the crest.

As we pushed toward the summit, we were nearing the spot where our "spring" was supposed to be, but it wasn't there. We spread out to look and both came back empty handed.

As great as digital mapping services are, we were both learning a tough lesson in tempering that trust. Having not been in situations like this before, we decided that we had to go into water rationing mode, slow down our movements, and figure out how to make a small amount of water last for the next day or two. We knew that our safety was reliant on this. I jokingly told my buddy that I wasn't planning to drag his tall ass out of those woods if we got heat exhaustion.

Sitting and staring into the hunting unit.

Joking through the pain, we slowly made it to the top of our mountain and spent the next few hours glassing the beautiful and empty region. We could see a few deer miles out, but nothing appeared close enough for us to tackle with our lack of water. Yet we both sat there smiling, dehydrated, and happy—we'd reached our destination.

Eventually we broke from our spot, as daylight was starting to fade fast, and we needed to make our way back down the steep mountain to where we had set up our camp.

Sitting on a ridgeline in camp with a stupidly tall friend, no light pollution, and only the sounds of distant animals to serenade us was otherworldly. That feeling of wonder was what drove me on these explorations. Yes, harvesting an animal is an amazing skill to acquire in itself, but the earthly *experiences* you gain deep in the backcountry are something you can't artificially create anywhere else. No Instagram posts, no social validation, and no amount of likes could ever replicate the feeling of being unreachable and fully alone in nature, exposing yourself to the raw power of a wild land. In that moment, my work as a corporate drone, my past mistakes as a husband, my countless ineptitudes as a human and partner, and even my future faded from thought as I gave in to just being present.

As we each sat there in our own deep and personal meditations, our concentration was acutely broken by the sound of loud "thunder" on a clear night. Looking around, we realized that to our north, a rockslide had given way, which moved a huge mass of earth in a split second. We silently acknowledged the violence that this place was capable of, chuckled that we were glad we didn't pick that area to camp, and turned in for the night.

As I lay under the stars, my mind went to a lot of different places. I thought of my new wife, our young daughter, and then my childhood best friend's mom.

Before we had set out for the hunting trip, I received a call from that longtime friend who informed me that his mother, a big influence during my formative youth, was suffering from COVID complications and was likely to be pulled off her ventilator within the next few days.

With no way to communicate now with my friend, I said a silent prayer that night under the stars. As cheesy as it sounds, shortly after that prayer, I saw a beautiful shooting star that illuminated the already bright night. I could feel in my soul that this woman, a second mother to me, had departed this Earth. In that moment, I felt close to her and to my best friend's family, yet they would never know.

I would sadly find out when we got home the next day that she did in fact pass away that evening, making that moment with her spirit all the more special.

I think about that night in the woods often, a time when I was able to intently focus and feel a connection to our world—to feel small and recognize that we are all just passengers on this planet. I recognized the sadness I feel for those who no longer get to experience life in the ways I was now able to.

The next morning, we decided to break camp early and journey home. We ran into a few deer and made a few unsuccessful stalks, sat and watched a few bighorn sheep in the distance, and slowly made our way back to the trailhead.

That season, we were both unsuccessful in the pursuit of harvesting a deer, but we both continued to gain woodsmanship knowledge. More importantly, we were gaining an understanding of who we were as people and what was important to us as individuals.

Hunting was not just about the pursuit of an animal but more about the experience itself, finding the space to process raw emotion. It gave us the chance to frame our complicated modern lives in a meaningful way.

8

ANTELOPE AND RATTLE SNAKES

Holy shit, General Custer! What happened?"

It was impossible not to notice the six arrows sticking in the ground at different angles around one lone sage bush. As my friend made his way toward me, I cautioned that there was a rattlesnake right where my arrows were.

Wounded but not dead, the aggressive snake that my boot nearly squashed ten minutes earlier was coiled and poised for a strike. I aimed the front sights of a 9mm sidearm at the serpent's diamond-shaped head and pulled the trigger.

We now had fresh meat for dinner.

It had only been a few days since I had picked up Blake, an old wrestling buddy and business partner, at the Boise airport. He was a proper southerner who had been deer hunting his whole life and had spent several trips hunting big game on the plains of Africa. I was excited he was joining me on this hunt so I could show him my new skills and the beautiful land that I now called home.

We had arrived in the rattlesnake-laden desert sage flats of the Pahsimeroi Valley, a beautiful and isolated spot shadowed by Idaho's tallest mountain peak, early on a Thursday morning. We had four days to try and close the distance on one of the most unique-looking and allegedly tasty mammals in the Pacific Northwest, the American antelope.

Having drawn an archery antelope tag for an either-sex controlled hunt, I could traverse three adjacent hunting units in search of this animal. Despite the large number of tags given for this particular hunt, the success rate was only 12 percent, and we were about to find out why.

Matching Wits with Antelope

We were excited as the wheels of our truck, hauling a small utility vehicle, crossed into the hunting unit. On either side of the road, we saw large herds of antelope with some males who could easily make it into the Pope and Young record books.

We would stop the car, pull out binoculars and spotting scopes, and sit in awe. These animals were so in tune with their environment that they could see great detail and small movements over a mile away and could spot our truck. As soon as one of our truck doors opened, they spooked and dispersed at breakneck speeds. Within seconds they were out of range and, shortly thereafter, out of sight.

For miles we would drive, keep coming up on new herds, and wind up spooking them. It was easy to find them, as all we had to do was drive slowly for a mile or so, and we would spot a new group. Yet no matter where we looked, there were no terrain features for us to hide behind.

Roadside antelope.

When I say this terrain was flat, I mean this terrain was a pancake. There were literally no bobbles or humps in the ground until you reached the mountains, which projected out of the earth to ten thousand feet in what seemed like just a few yards. To make matters more complicated, the only foliage and cover was sagebrush, which in this area only grew to be about shin high.

With three days and seemingly endless herds of antelope, we decided to give everything a try. Trial by error.

Our first tactic was to stop our vehicle in an area we thought was out of sight of a herd. I would grab my bow and walk painstakingly slow toward the antelope in an awkward half-crouch and hope that my fancy Sitka-brand camo would break up my pattern enough to just walk in on them. Stupid.

I took maybe fifteen steps before the herd bolted. Turning to my friend, we shared a laugh and decided we should scratch that approach off our list. Back into the truck we went as we pushed on to the next herd.

This time, my buddy got out of the truck and took a decoy of a female antelope form to block his shape. He walked in the field to try and draw their line of sight while I belly crawled (yes, this was before we knew this area was overrun with rattlesnakes) across the annoyingly flat terrain.

For the next hour, my buddy made antelope calls and jiggled his little decoy, which worked pretty well for a while. It didn't garner enough interest to bring any bucks in, but it hadn't yet scared them off. Within that hour, I had made just enough progress to get within two hundred yards of the group, which was only about one hundred and fifty yards away from a comfortable shooting range.

Like the elk I had hunted before, these antelope seemed to have a sixth sense that let the whole herd know there was something afoot whenever we were within a three-hundred-yard bubble. Within that bubble, you would see a few nostrils flare on some of the females, and the whole group would disappear at lightning speed.

I stood up and watched these speed demons jet off, turned to my buddy with a shoulder shrug, and we once again made the short walk back to the truck.

By this time, we decided we should find a spot to set up camp so we could hunt the last light and not have to fiddle with a tent in the dark afterwards. After some bumpy off-road driving, we found a gorgeous spot along a dried riverbed, which was littered with bleached animal bones, near the Donkey Hills in Custer County, Idaho.

Prior to this hunt, I had called to talk to the regional Idaho Fish and Game biologist, who filled me in on some of the antelope patterns in the region. He mentioned that most of the antelope bed up in the foothills at night and then work down into the flats and surrounding agriculture fields during the day.

Our plan was to camp near the hills, set up a hunting blind near a water source, and hopefully cut some of them off at first or last light. So after making camp, and with a few hours left of sunlight, we decided to go set up our blind, which was just a glorified plastic tent with a camo pattern. That patterned tent would allow us to sit relatively concealed as we waited for an animal to hopefully walk by within shooting range. In our case, however, this blind would mostly serve as a giant Easy-Bake Oven, slowly cooking us each day in the desert heat.

We found a spot near a small creek we thought would be a high traffic area for antelope, set up our mobile crematorium, logged the location on our digital maps, and went back to camp for the evening. As the sun began to set, we pointed our spotting scopes toward the hills to see if the regional biologist's information was accurate. Sure enough, he was spot on, and we began to see antelope in and out of the timber lines in the steep hills above us. This gave us some hope for our day two game plan, and we turned in for the night.

Sunset over our campsite.

Those optimistic dreams turned into a nightmare at about two that morning. Out of a deep sleep, I could feel adrenaline explode through my body as our remotely pitched tent was filled with the headlights of an oncoming truck. I could hear the diesel truck engine revving before we were blinded by the headlights in what we thought may be our last moments on Earth as we both lay stuck in a nylon coffin. I shot out of my sleeping bag and unzipped the front of our tent with such speed that even I was impressed. By the time I got up and out of the tent to see what was happening, I caught the taillights of a truck speeding away.

Confused and with near-spoiled underwear, we both collected our thoughts. In the middle of nowhere, on an unmarked road, we had almost been run over. We weren't quite sure if it was a drunken hunter, a rancher, or aliens testing some futuristic AI technology, but it certainly scared the absolute crap out of both of us.

For the next few hours, we fought to try and sleep again until we both gave up. With first light only a few hours away, we decided to get dressed, have some breakfast and coffee, and make the long, dark walk to our sitting blind. After a thirty-minute walk under a pitch-black night, we arrived at where we had left our blind the evening before, but as we walked up to our staked space, we were confused.

Our blind was gone!

Though our mapping service said we should be standing right on top of it, there was nothing. We shared some confused looks under the red light of our headlamps and started to break down what could have happened.

"You think someone stole it?" my friend whispered.

"Hell, maybe it was run over by the guy in the truck ripping around these fields in the middle of the night," I said.

We both agreed that the most likely scenario was that the winds had picked up on this Mars-like surface and blown our blind down the prairie. With literally no clue what to do, we naturally landed on the worst idea and turned on our bright lights to see if we could catch the shape of the blind against the horizon. As we turned them on and did a three-sixty, we were met by a sea of red eyes catching the light of our headlamps.

Dammit. We had stumbled into a mecca of antelope who were all bedded down, most of which were easily within bow range. Though we couldn't see, we could hear as one by one, those antelope trotted off to safer ground along with our hopes for the morning.

Running to set up our decoy.

To rub just a little more salt into our now gaping ego-wound, we walked less than four hundred yards and came right up on our completely undisturbed hunting blind. Our map had once again led us slightly astray, and that familiar reliance on technology cost us a first attempt at daybreak on the herd we had just spooked.

With equal parts frustration and dumb optimism, we kept our original plan. We set up our decoy antelope fifty yards from our blind and settled in for what we knew would be a long sit.

Looking out from our blind in the early morning.

Unlike the spot-and-stalk nature of most western hunts, we were employing something more akin to the tree-stand hunting that I had first learned back East. We would sit as silently as possible in our plastic-lined blind and pray that an antelope would be curious enough to come check out our decoy and walk to within fifty yards.

Despite our early morning herd spook, we actually had some action at daybreak. We watched in complete silence as three lone does came within three hundred yards of our blind. It seemed as though our decoy had caught their attention, and one bold doe began to close the distance.

As she crossed the two-hundred-yard threshold, I excitedly put an arrow on my rest. Simultaneously, my buddy slowly un-Velcroed one of our shooting windows on the side of the blind we expected this doe to come in on. At one hundred yards, I placed my bow release on my string and prepared myself to go through my shot sequence. At eighty yards, I used my range finder to confirm her distance and set my bow sight to the longest comfortable shooting distance I would take, sixty yards.

With just a measly twenty yards left for her to walk, she stopped.

The intense prayers I was sending up to the Big Man could not be understated: Twenty. More. Yards.

Realizing that she wasn't going to come any closer, I instinctively rolled the dial on my bow site to eighty yards and started to justify in my head that taking a shot *slightly* out of my comfortable range would be fine. The good demon/bad demon battle that I was facing in those moments was intense as I realized the success or failure of my hunt was riding on a few mere yards.

In my case, two things happened. First, the antelope I was staring at took another slow step toward eighty-two yards, then eighty-five yards, and stopped once again at ninety yards. Second, these steps gave my brain enough time to catch up to the hunting ethics I hold myself to and allowed my inner voice to remind me that wounding such a beautiful animal would be a senseless and selfish act.

Taking my arrow off the bowstring and placing it back in the quiver, we watched as these three antelope slowly walked away, giving no indication that they ever knew we were there.

For the next day and a half, we abandoned the boring sitting nature of the blind and opted for the high-pace, low-yield spot-and-stalk approach. Like day one, we would spy a group of antelope, crawl for hours, and ultimately never break the one-hundred-yard barrier. We did, however, get better on each stalk.

The beautiful thing about antelope hunting in this region is that you get repetition. You fail? Okay, just move on to the next group to try a slightly different approach. This masterclass lasted for hours without success.

Fear the Heel of Man

Later that evening, we were both exhausted from our day of chasing antelope and went back to our camp to regroup. Relaxing while eating a snack, I caught the sight of some errant antelope in the low rolling hills not too far from camp and decided I would chase after them. Leaving Blake behind, I grabbed one of our radios and set out on what became yet another failed attempt at closing the distance on an antelope.

Walking back to our camp about an hour later, my body reacted to the tiniest movement in the sagebrush that I was about to step through. It's impossible to articulate how quickly my brain reacted, but without conscious thought, I found myself jumping through the air on one foot while my heart simultaneously almost exploded through the front of my chest. When I landed, I was about two feet away from the coiled, three-foot-long rattlesnake I mentioned earlier. Had my body not reacted so quickly, the heel of my boot would have struck the snake mid-body, and I am sure I would have gotten a nice dual-fang tattoo on my lower calf.

I hate snakes with a passion. Not in the sense of "kill any snake I see," but holy crap, do they scare me. This goes all the way back to the biblical Old Testament, when God made the serpent and said that man will fear the snake, while the snake will fear the heel of man, and let me tell you, I had pure biblical fear at that moment.

What's interesting, though, is this snake never actually started to rattle to alert me of its presence, something I found a bit disappointing and unnerving in hindsight. I decided that with him being less than one hundred yards away from our campsite, he needed to go. I stood a mere eight yards away and took aim at his head with my bow. But as soon as my first arrow released, the snake somehow jumped the string and was able to maneuver with lightning speed out of the way.

Having never seen anything move so fast before, I put another arrow on my string and walked toward the back of the snake. Once again taking aim at his head, I released the arrow, and with Jedi-like reflexes, the snake once again avoided my shot.

This led me down the path of employing Sitting Bull's tactic during Custer's Last Stand: I ended up shooting all six of my arrows at this snake, with only one or two making connections with its body. With the snake now wounded and pissed off, I radioed Blake back at our camp to bring my pistol. After dispatching the snake, I collected my now dull and dirty arrows, and we made our way back to camp for our evening meal.

As we began to skin out the snake, we were unnerved by its body's ability to continue moving as if it were alive. With no head and no skin, the muscles would continue to contract and make the naked body of the snake contort in unnatural ways even after it had hit the frying pan—truly a creature of demonic descent.

Cutting off the snake's head and the tanned hide a few weeks later.

With a fresh meal down, a beautiful snakeskin to tan, and only a few hours left to hunt, we decided to call it early and break camp. On the long ride home, we chatted about how the experience of hunting antelope was not necessarily the highlight or focal point of our trip. Nature had a way of teaching us lessons we weren't expecting. We certainly weren't expecting to be dosed with the primal fear of nearly being run over by a truck *and* snakebit on our hunt, yet they were both lessons in caution that we clearly needed to learn.

9

BEAR

Have you ever heard a bear die? I have and it damn near broke my heart.

When a bear enters its final moments on this Earth, it lets out a soul-crushing moan that sounds as much pained as it does remorseful. Once heard, you will never forget it.

When I first arrived in Idaho, I had no idea about the death moan of a bear, nor did I know how abundant the species was in the state. The only thing I knew about bears was that they loved pots of honey and picnics, and they reminded me of my own large-breed dogs.

To be honest, hunting bears was not even on my radar when I arrived out West. It wasn't until I had my first in-person exposure to black bears that I began to consider the benefits of harvesting one.

Ignorant Bliss

My first encounter with the species was on my first elk hunt with the outfitter I described in Chapter 6. Between bouts of chasing elk all around the White Clouds Wilderness, we also had permanent visitors each and every night: black bears.

Without fail, I would hear the rustling of tarps at around two or three in the morning, the whinnies of the horses, followed by the sound of our guides' tents unzipping as they screamed and yelled. That was followed by the crashing and breaking of limbs like a staccato wilderness serenade as three hundred pounds of muscle would go crashing through the woods away from camp.

The guides would survey the damage to the horse feed, rewire the downed electric bear fence, and get back to bed.

This would happen at least twice a night, and you could see the annoyance, not fear, on our guides' faces every time it would happen.

The frequency of our visitors was partially because the black bear population is so healthy in Idaho, with over thirty thousand animals roaming the various mountain ranges. Every time I saw one, I was in awe at both their size and elegance in the woods. Yet my guide continually seemed more frustrated at their presence around camp.

Why?

Well, as it turns out, if you are running a business that is focused on hunting in the woods, and you need to support pack animals and food for guests, bears can be more than a pest. They can cut into your bottom line.

While we were out hunting during the day, bears would come into camp and try to tear through every "bear-proof" cooler and tent we had. It became so troublesome that one of our camp tenders would stay back just to shoo the bears away.

Despite the economic annoyance of losing a meal or horse feed, the majority of the bears we would encounter bolted as soon as we came into camp or when we started to scream at them. After a few close encounters, my heart rate eventually quit elevating when I would see a new bear.

Over just a few short days, my fear of these animals dwindled down to near zero, and I thought of them as no more than annoying, drunk friends who were trying to raid my fridge. A friendly holler would send them packing, and I had no reason to worry about them hurting me. Of course, this was ignorant bliss on my part and an unsafe mindset to have in the backcountry. It only takes one terrifying encounter with a bear to reshift your entire mental landscape, and my mind was surely about to get a major reset.

Coming back into camp from hunting on one of the later days on the elk hunt, we saw a familiar sight, an oversized, dark form darting off into the woods. That raised no alarm bells for our grizzled crew, and we went about unsaddling our horses and preparing for the evening.

As we dismounted, all of our eyes and ears caught something behind one of our wall tents. Like a comedy sketch, out walks an absolutely adorable bear cub with a look of curiosity on its face.

Completely unfazed by our presence, it started to go about its business rummaging through our campsite.

Caught off guard by the sheer cuteness of the brave little furball, I failed to see the reactions of our guides. In a matter of seconds, everyone around me had unholstered their sidearms and had their eyes intently glued not on the little cub but the woods surrounding camp.

Having not been exposed to bears throughout my life, I had limited knowledge to work from. The few things I had learned in bear 101 lessons included things like "If you encounter a bear, *do not run*," or "If you encounter a bear, *play dead*," and "Never, ever, get between a mama bear and her cubs."

Shit. That last one was surely in play now. Right on cue, I heard the first charge.

Unlike the sound of bears running away from camp at night, the sound of an amped-up and angry mama bear charging at your group was a terrifying experience. I could palpably feel the ground move with every frustrated stride she took and see every beautiful, rich, black hair standing up on her back in an aggressive display of dominance. My body reacted in kind (not out of aggression but fear) and forced goose bumps to appear, making all of my own body hairs stand on end. I could feel the blood draining from my face as she got to within thirty yards before hitting the brakes.

Between charges, she would retreat some distance, let out some deep guttural woofs, walk around to find a different angle of attack, and repeat the process. Meanwhile, her cub was happy as a clam, just farting around our camp as if nothing exciting was going on.

Angry mama bear circling camp.

Pretty quickly, the guides' attention turned to the cub. In the state of Idaho, it is illegal to kill a mother sow that is with cubs, so the only means to getting mama bear to leave us alone was to strongly encourage the little tyke to take a hike.

While one guide stood watch for the circling sow, the rest of us went to work on the cub. We started by tossing rocks in its direction, which went completely unanswered. That escalated to more yelling, stick waving, and eventually Western-cartoon-pistol firing to try and convince the little one to go sync up with its waiting mama.

Unnerved, the little cub started to approach one of the guides. With no options left, the guide decided to meet the cub in the middle with a swift kick. With NFL kicker precision, he lined his boot up with the approaching cub, and within a yard or two, wound up his right leg and gave the cub a kick in the left side that lifted him off the ground by a few inches.

Stunned, the little guy realized that we weren't up for sharing our food, and not in the mood to cuddle. The punt reset his brain, and he decided that maybe he should go see his mom. He trotted off toward the woodline.

The charges and woofing subsided. We all breathed a heavy sigh of relief as the sounds of our new friends were swallowed up by the surrounding pines.

That terrifying encounter piqued my curiosity about bears and predators in general. When I was home from that hunt, I did some research. I wanted to understand the process of bear hunting, the approach, and more importantly, how I could use the different parts of the animal. What I uncovered surprised me. There is a whole movement of people, most notably Clay Newcomb of MeatEater, who are pushing to educate the public on the benefits of harvesting the abundant black bear species. With over three hundred thousand black bears across the United States, and relatively strict harvest allowances, the bear population is on a steady growth trajectory. Aside from being an abundant and truly renewable resource, almost the entire animal is usable, and barely anything goes to waste.

The copious amounts of fat can be rendered down to a long-lasting and delicious oil to be used for cooking; the hide can be used for clothes, rugs, or blankets; and the meat is delicious and lean. Hunters can even use the bear penis (baculum), which is an actual bone, as a cocktail stirrer or general novelty.

That information was eye-opening to me, as I had previously assumed that the only reason for hunting bears was sport. Armed with this new knowledge, I purchased a bear tag and made the promise that if I had the opportunity to harvest a bear, I would honor it by utilizing everything it had to offer and process the animal by myself.

While I waited for the spring bear hunting season, I turned back to the internet to understand the best tactics for hunting bears with a bow and arrow. About the only thing I could surmise was that there was a lot of luck involved, as well as a lot of hiking. It also sounded like closing the distance on a bear without sitting in a tree stand was going to be a Herculean task, but as soon as the season opened on April 15, I was off.

Hey, Bear!

Luckily for me, Olesya and I had just had our first child not long before the season opened. With my paternity leave (a huge perk of the modern tech industry) in full swing, I was able to spend my mornings hiking as deep into the backcountry as possible, getting high up on ridgelines, which gave me views into the pine-rich draws below, where I would sit and glass for hours before heading home to help with the baby. That went on for days with my seeing nothing but distant deer and elk, two animals that were out of season and off-limits to pursue.

On the fifth day of hunting, I finally caught a glimpse of a beautiful black blob on a distant hillside that reminded me of the Rorschach tests I took as a kid. Ecstatic, I started to calculate how I might close the distance of such a large magnitude in order to get close enough with my bow. As I sat looking at my watch and calculating what pace I would need to set to close the distance, I took another look at the bear through my binoculars and had my hopes dashed. Trailing not too far behind her were two little black dots that were clearly her offspring, making her an illegal target.

Defeated, I headed out of the woods and sauntered back to our cabin.

The next morning, I awoke at my normal predawn time and went outside to grab wood to start a fire in our cabin's wood burning stoves. As I stepped toward our woodshed, my peripheral vision caught something strange on my left side. I noticed something distinctly white laying in our yard: one of my infant daughter's diapers. That was odd, as I had put all of our household trash into the back of my pickup the night before to take to the dump that very morning. When I went to investigate the diaper, I immediately saw another piece of trash not too far off. Without thinking, I followed the trail until I found a perfectly ripped trash bag with piles of fresh bear scat all around it.

Though it took me longer than I care to admit to understand what had caused the abstract trash art, it was now apparent to me that we had a very large and hungry visitor coming onto our property. As I picked up the garbage and made it back to the house, any doubts that lingered were put to rest when I saw a distinct, muddy bear-paw print on the white door of our workshop.

Excited, I ran inside to tell my wife, who was measurably less impressed with the news than I was. Grabbing my gear, I set out to try my best at tracking down and dispatching the intruder. Yet after a day of searching, I came upon no signs and was running only on blind ambition. When I returned home, I game-planned to head out again the next day. I was confident we would eventually meet up deep in the woods behind our cabin.

Yet the circumstances in which we would actually meet turned out to be nothing like the perfect movie I was playing in my head. At first light the next morning, my wife shook me awake with a jarringly loud whisper. "Zach, I think there is something outside!"

My new pioneer wife was not one to cry wolf, so when she alerted me to danger, I listened and jolted out of bed. I rubbed the sleep from my eyes, threw on some underwear, and prepared myself for whatever it was she had heard.

The noise Olesya picked up with her postpartum superpowers was coming from outside the French doors of our bedroom. As I slowly pulled back the curtains, it took my eyes a minute to adjust to the early morning light. With a few blinks to make sure I was seeing what my brain registered, there stood the bear who had tried to break into our house the day before. It was perfectly broadside at thirty-five yards. My gentle and usually curse-word-free wife was now peeking over my shoulder and excitedly screamed, "It's a bear; it's a fucking bear!" before quickly muzzling herself with her hand.

We both let our cortisol levels come back down to baseline before I grabbed my bow, which was hanging beside our bed.

We formulated a quick plan in which my wife would stand by our baby's crib, a mere two steps away, to make sure she didn't start screaming, while I would slowly open one of our doors and silently slip outside to see if I could make a shot.

With our plan hatched, we went into action. I placed an arrow on my string, attached my release, and set my bow sight to thirty-five yards. My wife took one large step backwards to tend to the baby, and then I slowly opened the door.

Stepping just outside, barefoot and in my underwear, I raised my bow. I was able to easily put my fluorescent-yellow aiming pin directly behind the bear's left shoulder and onto the vital-organ zone. Without him ever knowing I was there, I punched the release and let my arrow fly.

At the twang of my arrow string, the bear instinctively quartered slightly toward me, and my arrow entered just behind his shoulder at a slightly different angle than I intended. With a louder than expected woof, which echoed through the entire draw behind our home, he took off in the opposite direction of the impact, while my wife and I shared a disbelieving look.

It wasn't quite the way I had intended to take my first bear, but with a nearly empty freezer, we needed to embrace a somewhat opportunistic mindset. After our hearts made their way back to our chests, I set out to look for my arrow and for blood to ensure that I had a solid hit. At the impact site, I had a twinge of relief as I found the back half of my arrow with some decent blood on it, along with a clear trail of blood in the direction the bear ran.

Blood on the trail.

The only confusing fact was that my arrow was split in two, which meant that it likely impacted something hard, potentially the bear's shoulder bone. Knowing now that I did not have a clean passthrough of the vitals, I tempered the speed of my pursuit.

After being hit, the bear had taken a well-worn game trail that ran near the back of our house. As I followed the blood and excrement, it felt like I was playing an intricate game, one that was initially very easy. But after the first one hundred yards or so, the blood started to become less and less apparent. I followed it for as long as I could before I needed to go back home and recruit my wife to help her color-blind husband identify the red blood on the green spring foliage.

Strapping our infant child to her chest, my wife and I combed the area for the next hour, marking tiny blood splatters with orange flagging tape as if we were canvassing a crime scene on *NCIS*. Step by step, we would get down on all fours and search for blood. The diminishing blood eventually led us down a steep hill toward the base of an even larger hill that opened up in all directions, which is where we lost the signs.

The hillside where we lost our bear.

It was as if the bear had vanished into thin air.

We had a very clear trail up to that point, and it just stopped cold. There was no indication of which direction the bear took, and the options were numerous. The visions I had in my head of taking a picture with my first archery bear started to quickly fade away and transform into dread and self-doubt.

Had I missed the bear? Did I hit a bone and only wound it? How far did this bear run?

And then it started to rain. Any sign of blood that we may still have been able to find was being washed away in front of our eyes. My stomach started to knot up.

With the rain becoming heavier, Olesya went back to the house with our baby, while I continued to crawl on hands and knees, putting myself in the mindset of the wounded bear I was failing to track.

After some time, my wife was able to secure childcare for the rest of the day and came back to join me with water and snacks. Together we both sat in the rain, looking up at the enormous expanse of land that lay before us. She consoled me and assured me that we would not give up looking for that bear and rightly said, "We owe it to the animal." The assurances only slightly assuaged my concern. But as if the bear had heard us talking, there came a guttural death moan from somewhere out on that open hillside.

It was hard to distinguish exactly where it came from, but in that moment, we knew our bear was out there. He had been kind enough to let us know as he passed on from this Earth. The sadness in that moan took us both by surprise. My wife openly cried. The rain masked my own tears welling in the corners of my eyes. Relieved that we had some rough coordinates, we went back home to call some friends to help us on our search.

Once our friends arrived, we set out to walk every square inch of the ridiculously steep and tall hillside where our bear had breathed its last breath. We took it in sections, each of us knocking through head-high chaparral while yelling out, "Hey, bear!" at the top of our lungs. Though we were convinced the bear had expired, we wanted to take every precaution, in case one of us stumbled upon a wounded and defensive bear.

That exercise went on for hours. We would climb and descend, climb and descend, until we were eventually dispersed by a passing thunderstorm, which sent us all back to the house in retreat from the cloud-to-ground lightning.

With each passing hour, more color faded from my face. Not only was I worried about finding the bear, but if the search dragged on much longer, the meat could spoil. Had I needlessly killed this animal for nothing? Guilt and disgust with myself were building by the minute.

Eventually our friends had to leave, and it was down to just me. Until well after dark, I worked that mountainside, praying for God to give me any sign as to where that animal may lay.

If I didn't find the bear by early the next day, we could kiss that meat goodbye.

At first light, almost twenty-four hours after I took the shot, another friend arrived to help me in my search. We followed the bear's route and got to where we had last seen blood. With a new set of eyes, we decided that if the bear were injured, he would likely not go far from that point and probably took the path of least resistance.

With that in mind, we walked straight up the hill one more time, and God came through for me. On that short walk and within less than two hundred yards, I heard my friend yell out, "Here he is!"

Running over, I laid eyes on the bear that I so desperately wanted to find. However, there was no elation at that moment for me, only the extreme relief of finding him.

My buddy asked if I needed any help in the skinning, and I said no. I needed time alone with that bear, to talk with it, and to see if I could salvage any meat. By that point, I had come a long way in my abilities to field dress and skin an animal, and seeing that I was planning to tan this bear hide on my own, it would be vital that I took my time and made all of the appropriate cuts with care.

My first archery black bear.

Field Dressing A Bear

As my buddy began to walk away in the dewy spring morning, I said a prayer of thanks, opened my knife kit, and began to work. For the next four hours, I worked like a surgeon. I had zero distractions, other than my wife occasionally visiting to bring some water and snap a few pictures.

One of the amazing things about field dressing and skinning an animal is that you can piece together what exactly happened when you shot it. Upon examining the bear, I was able to determine that my arrow had hit right where I expected, just behind the left shoulder. As the bear had quartered toward me, my arrow had slightly nicked the shoulder bone, breaking the arrow in half. The remaining piece of the arrow had taken a sharp right turn and traveled down through the bear's intestines, broken through the gallbladder, and ultimately ended up lodged in his testicles.

Removing the broadhead and arrow from his sex organs was actually trickier than it sounds because in the state of Idaho, you have to leave evidence of sex (testes for males and vulva for females) naturally attached to the hide for a mandatory check-in within ten days of a kill.

With some awkward knife maneuvering, I was able to successfully retrieve the arrowhead and kept working.

To my ultimate dismay, given the time it took for me to recover the bear, along with the gutshot and the heat of the prior day, most of the meat had spoiled. I was only able to preserve both hind quarters, the hide, baculum, and skull. With my loot prepared, I loaded up my pack and made my way home, feeling the weight of those past two days on my shoulders.

Back at the cabin, I unpacked the hindquarters, cleaned them up, wrapped them in plastic wrap and butcher paper, and put them in the freezer in anticipation of smoking the meat at a later date. Then I focused on the hide, which would quickly turn into a labor of love and a crash course in large-game animal hide tanning.

To start the process, I would have to do something that is usually reserved for expert taxidermists: deboning the feet.

Skinned and packed out: boning out the bear paws in my shop.

With an animal like a bear, most hunters leave the bones of the foot in the hide for a professional taxidermist to deal with later. I had done the same in the field, but since I was processing the hide myself, I would have to remove each finger and toe from the pads of the bear paw without disturbing or poking holes in the soft pad itself.

After three hours of cutting millimeter by millimeter, I was able to eventually remove each foot from the surrounding pad and nail structure. I couldn't help but feel like Dexter as I cut away at the thin layers of flesh holding the bone in place. It didn't help that the bone structure of a bear's paws is uncannily human-like when the furry outer protective layer is removed.

My wife and I spent the next two days trimming every bit of fat that we could off the hide. That sounds easy, but with razor blades, we would cut small globules of fat away for hours at a time. Whenever we thought we were done, more would seem to magically appear, until we finally had to call it good enough when our hide took on a bluish hue.

We then applied copious amounts of salt to dry the hide for forty-eight hours before I took on the chemistry experiment that is hide tanning. It's worth noting that in high school, I barely passed chemistry, but I quickly found myself wishing I had paid more attention in school to pH balance and acidity levels.

To start the tanning process, we took our salted hide and essentially pickled it. But instead of using a giant mason jar, we had some large plastic totes to do the job. In a solution that was 1:1 distilled white vinegar and water, we let our hide soak for six days.

On the sixth day, we set up a number of "baths" to take our hide through. First was a quick soak in a mixture of water and baking soda to kill the acidity of the pickling solution. That was followed by an even quicker dip in a water and bleach solution to kill any remaining bacteria that might have been on the hide. The rest were cycles of water and dish soap to clean off the dirt and hopefully give the fur a nice fresh scent.

Standing with my pickled bear hide.

Once it was washed a few times, it was back to the table for the actual tanning process.

In the old days, westerners would tan their hides with the brains of the animals they killed (it's pretty cool, and you should look it up), but I was going to leverage more modern household chemicals to do the job. With the now-clean bear hide laid out, I pulled out some neatsfoot oil, which is typically used for horses and can be bought at any tractor supply store, and made a solution of one part hot water to one part neatsfoot oil. But with oil and water doing what they do best—not combining—I needed an emulsifier.

I mixed in one tablespoon of dish soap, whisked the concoction, and spread it all over the hide. We then flipped the hide over to skin-side down on the table to allow the tannins to soak in overnight.

For the next several days, the hide began to dry, and during that time, my wife and I would break it in. We would pull, stretch, and rub it down with pumice stones to slowly and incrementally transform the hardening skin into a soft and supple leather. Inch by inch, we started to see the fruits of our labor as this beautiful hide turned into a warm blanket that our family could use for generations.

Satisfied that we had honored the bear's sacrifice sufficiently, we finally relaxed.

Four weeks of intense labor to process the animal was not a small commitment. It taught us a lot about the values we hold when we take an animal's life. It reaffirmed our family's promise to never give up searching for any animal that we take a shot at, and if we are ever in a position to take an animal's life, then we *will* do everything in our power to recover, process, and honor that animal.

PART III

TRAPPING

Learning is serial incompetence on the way to mastery.

—SETH GODIN

10

SQUIRREL AND MARTEN

I am not one who has ever been great at receiving gifts, but this one was different. Just looking at the wrapped box brought me a sense of childlike glee. It was from my new wife, Olesya, the mother of my children, and the woman who had bravely joined me on my great Western experiment.

As the paper peeled back, I could start to see what was inside: a deeply set frame, a shadow box.

As the final bits of paper were ripped away, I tried to make out what it was displaying, and a smile crept across my face as I realized what she had done.

The squirrel shadow box.

Ever the jokester, she had framed the first tanned hides I had attempted when we got to the backcountry. Three medium-sized tree-squirrel hides now looked like crinkled-up field mice that had been chewed on by a large dog. Those hides had been an astonishingly terrible job that could have been entered into the horrifying taxidermy hall of fame, but it was a great reminder of how far I had come.

Those little guys were my first foray into the art of skinning an animal and using tannins to convert their pelts into supple leather for use in clothing. Anyway, that had been my intention.

When we first moved to our cabin, I had my eyes set on large game to hunt and prize-winning furbearers to catch. My dreams were deep in the backwoods and would require time to study and a financial investment in the necessary equipment to ethically harvest them.

I would sit and think about these things on our front porch during the first early spring and would find myself distracted by the constant chirping of ground squirrels in the woods around us. During one of those irritating concerts, I thought back to my first exposure to hunting as an adult. At my ex-wife's family squirrel hunt back in Tennessee, I remembered seeing piles of squirrels ready for donation to feed the local homeless population. I'd also overheard conversations about culling the over-populated species. I remember thinking how silly the whole effort was.

Well, that was then, but in my current reality, I had to laugh out loud at the seismic shift of my opinions over such a short time-frame. As I sat there in my chair, mulling over the past opportunities I had missed out on, I decided I would start small and pursue some of the woodland critters that were cruising around our own property, which would ultimately be the basis for the shadow box my wife would eventually gift me.

So, without telling Olesya, I fetched my .22 rifle and went to work hunting my first squirrels.

Scouting Squirrel

I started to march around our property like a continental soldier, rifle slung over my shoulder, looking for the vocal squirrels that were constantly barking. My exuberance turned to frustration pretty quickly, as I realized these wily little things are harder to hunt than I expected.

Though you could hear them everywhere, it was hard to actually get eyes on them. Once you would see one and pull up your rifle scope, they would make some jerky crackhead movements and scurry around to the back side of the tree. To my wife, who did not know what I was up to, I probably looked hilarious. Just a guy walking aimlessly around the yard, looking up as if a meteor could hit at any moment, constantly raising and lowering his rifle.

I ended up retreating back to my front-porch chair to think up a new strategy, when I heard some squirrels barking in the tree beside me. With the same stealthy movement I would use for large game such as elk, I slowly grabbed the rifle laying at my feet and brought it up to my chest.

There was a beautiful squirrel sitting on a branch less than thirty yards away who was making continued quick movements of her forepaws. I continued to raise my rifle until I was looking through the crosshairs of my scope. The first thing I noticed were the extended tufts of hair coming off the ears and the squirrel's manic movement. As she turned to face me, I slowly put my finger on the trigger and focused on the crosshairs. With a releasing breath, I pulled the trigger, heard the audible pop of the gun, and saw the squirrel fall out of the frame of my scope. The low thud on the ground let me know I had met my mark.

I didn't retrieve my kill right away. Honestly, I felt bad for taking that squirrel's life, though I knew her purpose was to teach me how to remove skin from muscle. Instead, I pulled out my phone and watched how-to videos on skinning squirrels. Apparently there are dozens of methods, and much debate depending on the region where you live.

Skinning Squirrel

There was the "stand on the tail and pull" method, the "tube sock" method, and some that even required that you soak them in water before pulling back the hide. I opted to skin her out using the method for large-game animals that my buddy Alex and I first learned on a white-tailed deer back in Tennessee (see Chapter 4). I would cut from the anus up to the neck, and then down each appendage to meet up with my center cut. Then I would slowly peel the fur back around toward the spine and over the head.

I had a plan. After watching a few videos to refresh my memory, and to further procrastinate against the inevitable, I got up to grab my kill. I was surprised at how much blood there was for such a small animal, which did not help my feelings of sadness for this little critter.

I picked her up by the back foot and started to look at her in detail. The ears I saw in my scope were larger than I had anticipated, and her white belly was beautiful and contrasted by the red blood stains that now speckled it.

I then noticed some small black dots all over the squirrel. As I pulled her closer to my face, I felt as if my eyes were playing tricks on me as the dots began to move. Pulling it closer yet, I realized that this squirrel was absolutely riddled with fleas. This sent an uncontrolled shiver down my spine. I dropped the squirrel in disgust and went inside my workshop to put on some latex gloves.

It turns out that wild game animals do not follow the same regimen of flea and tick control that my house dogs do. No monthly pills to keep the itching at bay, just a hard and itchy life out in the elements.

I took her hand in glove to my workshop to attempt skinning my first small game animal. My palms were sweaty, accentuated by the gloves I was wearing. I could feel the sweat smushing up against the latex as I grabbed my knife and stood over the squirrel.

Under the shop light hanging above my table, it looked as if I were in an operating room and this squirrel had just been anesthetized. Grabbing her by the back legs, I started my first cut. Like the first deer I'd had to field dress on my own, I was surprised by the elasticity of the skin and how difficult it was for my knife to penetrate it.

Thinking that maybe my knife was dull, I took some time to sharpen it before trying again. With more pressure this go-round, I was able to punch through and get the first cut flowing. As I ran my knife up the belly, I made a mistake that many first-time hunters and trappers do, which is to perforate the guts. As I hit them, the small intestine of this tiny animal forced its way out of the cavity and covered the lower quarter of my knife.

Instinctively, I pulled away as the intestines set in along with the smell. Regretting my poor skills, I had to move the intestines to the side to find where I had left off with my cut. I was able to finish it out with a wee bit more finesse and successfully cut down all four limbs as well.

I was surprised to find that once the skin had been loosened, I was able to peel the rest off with relative ease. Starting at the head, I peeled the skin on the spine side like Velcro, all the way down to the squirrel's butt.

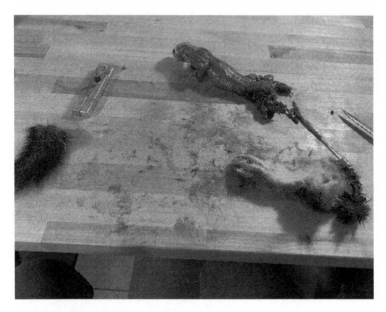

First bloody attempt at squirrel skinning.

The skin near the flanks became a little more tough to pull, which required a bit more strength. With the bare squirrel carcass in one hand and the pelt in the other, I pulled it hard to set it free. This worked well, but my aggressive tug had pulled the pelt clear away from the fluffy tail that was now detached from the body. Had I been more seasoned, I would have used a specialized tool called a "tail stripper" to delicately pull the tailbone from the fur, while still being attached to the body of the pelt.

Shit. With the pelt now free from the carcass, I went to work removing any bits of meat or fat that may have been left on the hide. Thankfully, squirrels are not very fatty animals and don't require too much fleshing.

I then set about finding a board to "pin" the squirrel hide to in order for it to dry out. I tried my best to recreate the shape of the squirrel, but my amateur approach was made apparent as my tailless squirrel looked like a furry Christmas tree pinned to that board. More relieved than satisfied, I decided to call my first attempt good before trying to harvest more squirrels the following day.

Tanning Squirrel

Throughout that next week, I became a real squirrel killer. I would take my dogs in the back and use them to locate the loud but hard-to-find squirrels. By the third kill, I was finally getting decent enough at skinning to have a fully intact hide with tail included. Satisfied with the small amount of meat and few pelts, I hung up my gun and decided to try my hand at tanning.

Following some YouTube guidance, I salted each pelt for forty-eight hours, which included scraping and resalting them at the twenty-four-hour mark. Then came the "soak."

I was supposed to make a saltwater solution to soak the pelts, which required bringing a brine to a boil, then letting it cool down to room temperature. What I failed to do, however, was clearly listen to the instructions.

Instead, I brought my saltwater to a low rolling boil, threw my pelts directly into the hot cauldron, and walked away for a few hours. When I proudly returned to my pot, I was expecting to pull out a nice pliable pelt that would be ready for a tanning. Instead, I pulled out three shrunken and unrecognizable pieces of leather. My full-size squirrel pelts now looked like mummified field mice. Confused, I went back to my YouTube educator to see where I went wrong and quickly realized my mistake. With shame, I showed Olesya my latest blunder. We both chuckled and went about our days.

It was a few months later that I was presented with the beautiful gift my wife had created. The "infamous" shadow box with my meager squirrel pelts would forever hang on my wall as a reminder of my initial incompetence as a half-assed backwoods taxidermist.

Marten Trapping

With those hard-learned lessons out of the way, I decided to set my sights on other small game in our area. Specifically, I was determined to trap marten, a voracious nocturnal carnivore that frequented the pine forests around us. A marten is a beautiful creature that resembles a weasel and has an amazingly thick coat during the winter months that produces a luxurious pelt.

Trapping those animals is more involved than shooting squirrels since they will rarely, if ever, come out during the day. Trapping martens involves the construction of special marten boxes to be set in trees and lure them into lethal body-gripping traps.

I had first come to learn about marten boxes for trapping on my walks in the woods during the summer months. I'd noticed several rectangular wooden boxes with a wire-mesh backing, nailed to random trees.

At our one and only town bar, I asked a few locals what those boxes were used for and received my first impromptu lesson in marten trapping. It turned out that years before I moved to my new town, there had been one or two trappers that frequented the woods of the area, sometimes leaving their empty marten boxes behind in high-catch areas.

That was great for me, as I now knew where martens were likely to be found, and I had a model for how to build my traps. I took a tape measure to one of those areas, got the dimensions, and set about building some of my own. With a little redneck engineering and woodworking, I had three workable marten traps ready to be placed in the woods before the season opened.

To my surprise, those little boxes are hard to wrangle into the backcountry. They are gangly, awkward, and surprisingly heavy. They also need to be drilled or nailed to a tree at an angle that will allow a marten to access the bait that lies in the back of the trap.

After a lot of sweating, heaving, and cursing, I was able to get all three traps out and set before winter came and the marten season began. When December did finally roll around, I took some rotten beaver meat, which apparently marten love, and headed out for the woods. What I did not account for, though, was the fact that we had received heavy snow, and I had not marked where my traps were with anything easily identifiable.

I knew roughly the location of all three boxes, but the several feet of snow made pinpointing them quite the challenge in the snow-laden pine boughs. I spent two days just kicking around snow trying to find where they were. In the process, I learned another vital lesson in preparation: mark my trap locations.

A couple of homemade marten boxes.

When I finally found them, I baited my traps by placing some painfully stinky rotted beaver meat at the back of the device, set my body trap conibear at the front, and called it good. For the next several days, I would snowmobile and then snowshoe out to my traps to check them with anticipation, but each day turned up with nothing.

Back at the town bar, one of the old-timers had told me, "Zach, marten are stupid and the easiest animal to catch," yet I continued to come up short. This was starting to make me wonder if I was the stupid one in this equation.

Despite the self-doubt, my persistence did eventually pay off, when I walked up to one of my traps and saw what looked like a brown ferret hanging from the contraption. Lured in by the beaver meat, it had tried to work its way past the body-gripping trap and met a very quick and painless demise.

The work I had previously undertaken trying to learn to skin and tan squirrels prepared me for working with the more valuable and delicate pelt of a Rocky Mountain pine marten. I was able to get the pelt loose with little issue and eventually had it dried and tanned in short order.

It would be a pelt I cherished, as it was the first and last marten I caught in my first season. When I talked to the old-timer again, he openly claimed that I must have been doing something wrong, as either the martens had become a bit more intellectual over the last decade or the caliber of trapping had dropped off.

I knew the answer to that question but was nonetheless proud of my single catch. After some alcohol-induced convincing, the old-timer agreed to go out with me during the next season to teach me some tricks and hopefully increase my future fur yield.

These types of selfless offers by experienced hands to teach me were a win-win for me. Instead of sitting at my laptop watching YouTube videos on trapping techniques between meetings about the newest AI algorithm we were building at work, I was able to actually get out in the woods with a teacher. The dichotomy of a fully remote work life, in which I rarely interacted with anyone in person, and the calloused, hands-on approach to my trapping endeavors was not lost on me. In fact, it was something I was growing to appreciate more each and every day. I found myself irritable on any day that passed when I didn't find dirt on my hands.

11

BEAVER

Flipping to the back of *American Trapper* magazine, I hastily grabbed my scissors and cut out an order form for a book collection by the modern American trapping legend Tom Miranda. It reminded me of ordering baseball cards in my childhood, and it was my first monetary commitment to thoughtfully learn the art of beaver trapping.

My fascination with this animal stemmed from its connection to westward expansion in the 1800s. It was the beaver's pelt, both warm and waterproof, that European fashionistas clambered for, and the beaver's castoreum glands that provided the unique scents for perfumes worldwide.

To get these items to market, it was the beaver trappers who would have to put their lives on the line, fighting harsh winters and hostile Indigenous populations. Those men and women fur trappers pushed the bounds of exploration for both adventure and fortune.

Nostalgia had taken root in my heart to learn this trade, but modern practicality also presented itself as I began to research what constituted the modern-day beaver trapper.

Although beavers are not as abundant as they once were, there are still huge populations sporadically spread throughout our country. With those populations left unchecked, and fewer people taking up the beaver-trapping trade, they often cause pricey ecological damage and are considered to be a nuisance species, much like nutria rats in the South.

Tree downed on our road by a beaver.

Their dams are engineered to flood lowlands in order to give them safe underwater channels to swim through, which manifests itself in flooded roads, clogged hydroelectric dams, and frustrated landowners. Without modern-day beaver trappers, this species would quickly overtake landscapes and cause irreparable damage to common utilities that we all enjoy.

Learning about the impacts that beavers had in my area alone made me excited to get started, but I was also naive. My first thoughts of beaver trapping were *how hard could this be?* I figured you just place a trap, put out some lure, and the beavers would just start stacking themselves up. But boy was I wrong.

First and foremost, there were many things I had to learn about the traps themselves that are used to capture beavers, including foothold traps, snares, and conibears—each one with different techniques to implement. So, as a first step before getting Tom's book in the mail, I went to a local trapping supply store to equip myself.

Trap Shopping

Walking into the store, I had no clue what I was doing or truly even looking for. Thankfully, the ladies running the joint (yes, ladies) were extremely helpful and pointed me in the right direction. They set me up with everything they thought I may need to get started in beaver trapping. That included foothold traps, drowning wires, conibears, and even beaver-hide stretchers. It also included my first whiff of a "lure" room, which my nose is still recovering from.

Local Idaho trapping supply store.

That lure room was a floor-to-ceiling enclosure that housed every type of animal gland and urine you could ever possibly need, and it smelled just like you would imagine. Holding my breath long enough to grab some beaver castoreum oil from one of the back shelves, I bolted from the room with my loot, paid, and went home to plan.

Handling those newly bought live traps for the first time was petrifying. None of the heavy-gauge steel contraptions came with instructions, and they each held so much kinetic power that it was intimidating. To build my confidence up, I again referred to my old friend YouTube to educate myself on how to set these suckers and give them a proper test run.

Sitting in my workshop and watching videos of trappers easily setting their equipment by hand gave me false confidence to make my first attempt at opening the jaws of a foothold trap. But my manhood was quickly eviscerated as I tried to muscle it open with all of my hand strength. I felt like a child trying to arm wrestle their father while he sits there laughing. I was also wary of the contraption snapping back on my hand.

It ultimately took a few days, many failed attempts, and several close calls, but I was eventually able to open and set each one of the new traps with all of my fingers still intact. Once I had the basics down, I spent many a nervous hour practicing different setting techniques in my workshop until I became comfortable handling and setting those trapping tools in any situation.

Then, on a snowy Tuesday, our intrepid mailman showed up with my book set. Like a kid, I hopped out to meet him in the driveway. Once he handed me the prize, I barely gave him time to say goodbye before I was off to dive into the pages.

Setting Beaver Traps

Boiled down to the most basic concepts, the book said that beaver trappers need to find water channels where beavers frequently swim, and set traps near entrances to their lodges, natural channels, and shoreline exit points. Another common "beaver set" is to break an active dam and place a trap near the site, then hope that a beaver will get so annoyed with the leak that they come to fix it and step onto a foothold trap connected to a drowning wire.

Tom Miranda and his twenty-dollar set of books had me fully believing that this was going to be easy. So, with a pair of cheap,

uninsulated waders, my traps, and beaver lure, I loaded up my
snowmobile to head upriver to a spot where I had found beaver
signs during the summer. With all sorts of unwarranted confidence, I made my way to the snow-covered area, stomped out a
path to the riverbank, and waded into the water.

Freezing my gonads off, I busted through a few inches of ice to
start finding channels that beavers may be using to travel. Not
knowing what those channels actually looked like made it difficult, but I pretended I was a beaver and picked out areas that I
would have liked to swim in. I put out some traps just like Tom
taught me in his book, surveyed my job, and then sat on the riverbank to enjoy some coffee and the beautiful scenery. I had no
reason to *not* believe that when I came back the next day, all of
my traps would be full of beavers.

My confidence was partially justified because when I did come back,
some of the traps *were* fired off. They just didn't have any beavers
in them. Of the many mistakes I would later realize I was making, I
had set traps directly in the main river's flow, which caused ice and
debris to pass right through my traps and set them off.

I quickly went about resetting the traps in a slightly different
order and even moved some of them upriver to different locations. That ineptitude went on for three to four weeks. Then all
of a sudden, the beaver-catching season was over, and I had not
caught a single one. To make matters worse, on the last day of the
season, while pulling my traps out of the water, I saw a beaver
staring at me from the shoreline. Though I can't confirm it, I am
pretty sure he was laughing and flipping me the bird.

Defeated and cold, I vowed to spend the next nine months
researching what it really meant to be a modern beaver

trapper. I ended up purchasing every book and watched every video on beaver trapping, including trapping memoirs from the 1800s to modern write-ups from celebrity trappers like Steven Rinella.

I would sit in my workshop day in and day out, rehashing everything I had done wrong, and focus on perfecting my trap setups for the following year. I would boil and dye my old traps, rig new foothold drowning wires, and exercise my olfactory glands with different types of castor-based lures.

More than once, Olesya would walk downstairs and find me with Rube Goldberg–esque experiments running constantly, testing what my trap would do when something stepped in it. I wanted to be sure that if I did connect on a beaver the following season, its demise would be quick and lethal. While performing these experiments in the off months, I also had time to think about the philosophy and morality of what I was trying to do.

My new father-in-law, who was a very religious man, brought to my attention on a weekend visit to our cabin some of what the Bible said about consuming the flesh of trapped animals. He pointed out that in Acts, chapter 15, there are clear instructions to abstain from sexual immorality, blood, and from anything that has been strangled. The latter two points are what concerned my father-in-law, as he knew we had every intention of eating the meat of the beavers and other animals we planned to trap.

I am not a strict interpreter of biblical laws and teachings, and I assumed this passage was a product of times when trapped or butchered animals did not get refrigerated or taken care of in a quick and hygienic manner, so it seemed to me an elementary instruction to avoid unnecessary sickness. Nonetheless, it made me think. Where do we draw the line between what is and isn't okay to consume?

After much thinking between my engineering experiments, I decided that it was more important for our family to honor any soul that we take by using as much of the animal as possible and, when safe, consume its flesh. Thanks to those near-constant trap tests and philosophical musings, by the time the following November rolled around, I was both mentally and physically ready to find success in the water.

So ready, in fact, that I was out on the first day of the season at a large, active beaver lodge I had found during the fall. The dams they had built were about to flood the forest service road they were built against.

Beaver-Trapping Season Two

Like a master chef, I worked that area like I was making an intricate dish. I created a full menu of different trap sets with several well-placed conibears, dam-break sets, and a few footholds to round it out. With nine traps out, I was positive with 100 percent certainty that I would be getting a beaver that day.

That evening I slept soundly, and as soon as I awoke before first light, I was in my truck, driving the seventeen miles to the beaver lodge to check traps. Getting close to the area, I could feel my heart racing, and I knew that I would soon be coming up on something that meant so much to me. I desperately wanted to exceed my first-season capabilities as a trapper, a goal that had occupied a huge portion of my brain space for the past several months.

Hopping out of the truck with my waders on, I pulled out my binoculars to get an early glance at some of my traps, and I saw nothing. Four out of the nine traps that I could see were completely untouched. Though that hit me hard, I still had faith that the other five traps that were out of sight might still hold beavers.

I practically fell down the steep embankment in anticipation and crawled up and over a huge downed tree to step onto the dam. To my joy, I could tell that two of my dam-break sets had been triggered! Yet when I got up to them, they were empty. To throw salt on the wound, the beavers had completely repaired the dam *around* my traps.

That was the same scenario at all of my other sets too, including the traps that I had set directly in front of their lodge entrance. Stopping to compose myself, I couldn't help but laugh while I openly asked myself, "How are these critters so much smarter than me?"

I had studied this animal so well, done exploratory fieldwork, and engineered what I thought were slam-dunk sets, and still nothing. Bloated with humble pie yet again, I was worried that the area may be blown, as animals can quickly become conditioned to trapping approaches and become nearly impossible to catch.

Despite that concern, I decided to reset my traps and try a few new techniques. I moved my conibear body traps to shallower travel paths and made new dam breaks for my footholds. Feeling confident in the tweaks I made based on how they had found my last traps, I packed up and went home.

For the next twenty-four hours, I would try to understand how those animals were able to be one step ahead of me at every turn. When first light hit, I was back on the road.

I pulled up to the lodge just as the sun began to crest over the surrounding mountain peaks, and again pulled out my binoculars. This time, however, I was caught off guard. Through the lenses, I could see a shape in the water where one of my body-grip traps was placed. In disbelief, I had to adjust the clarity on my binoculars several times before the realization set in that the shape sticking out of the water was a beaver tail!

Rushing down to the water, I made my way to the trap. Sure enough, there was a beautiful, medium-sized female beaver perfectly and humanely caught in the trap.

Pulling her out of the water was mesmerizing, as I had never been up close to a beaver before that experience. The digital-only interactions I'd had with beavers through videos and stories were becoming a reality. With gratitude swelling my heart, I sat on the bank, examining that creature, feeling a direct connection to all of the men and women who had inspired my youth. They'd risked their lives to move west just to capture these prehistoric-looking animals, and to make a better life for themselves.

The first thing I noticed were her teeth. Yellowed and rounded, they felt and looked as though they could easily cut through steel. She had rodent-like facial features and front paws that resembled a small dog. The thick fur covering her round belly led to her duck-like back feet and her scaly platypus tail.

That creature looked like a mashup of odd animals packaged into one underwater nocturnal rat.

Trapped beaver and dried pelts.

After more examination and contemplation, I decided to check my other traps, all of which were untouched and empty.

I hauled my catch up the steep ravine and gained an appreciation for how hefty these animals can be. I then gently placed her in the bed of my truck and raced home to show my wife, and to begin processing my very first Rocky Mountain beaver before having to attend my first work call of the day at nine that morning.

Processing Beaver

After a few pictures, I busted out my new leather skinning apron and got a table ready. I had watched countless skinning videos from the *Coon Creek Outdoors* YouTube channel during the offseason and was ready to rock 'n' roll. I knew that processing that fur and saving the meat, skull, baculum, and castor glands was going to be a chore.

Taking each cut with slow, methodical precision, I started to separate the skin from the meat, working from the tail up to the belly, then down each side toward the spine to expose her beautiful pink-tinged meat that closely resembled pork. Thankfully, beavers are a fatty animal with thick skin, which made my novice knife work less of a burden, as it was harder to put a hole in the hide with my frequent slipups.

First beaver skinning.

After about two hours (a professional fur handler can do this work in less than twenty minutes), I had finally processed my first beaver. I had a beautiful hide that I would be making into a blanket for my daughter, meat for us to cook into pulled BBQ beaver sandwiches, and glands and a skull to sell for a small profit.

Fresh beaver meat turned into pulled BBQ beaver sandwiches.

After placing the fur on a metal ring to dry, I sat back to reflect on the effort required to catch just one beaver. My appreciation for what our ancestors had to endure to make a living, and for what professional fur handlers still have to do to this day, made me so thankful for the experience that animal had given me.

What's even better is that I had also finally hit my stride after years of experimentation. For the next few weeks, before heavy snow set in, I was able to stack up the nuisance beaver that had been plaguing a busy section of our road. Every time I set a trap, I would analyze the terrain and place it in the optimal spot, and each time, I would hit the mark and catch another beaver, some tipping the scales at over fifty pounds.

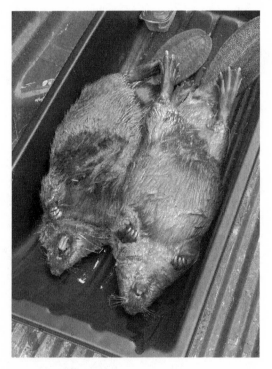

A couple of large beavers.

That spate of success was the closest thing I had felt to finding a flow state in trapping or hunting—something I had only achieved previously in athletic and business endeavors. I felt so close to the animals I was catching that I began to feel as if I could anticipate and intuit their movements.

My season would eventually come to an end, and for my efforts, we had many beautiful waterproof pelts to show for it, as well as a very full freezer of meat. I was able to end the season with a hard-earned knowledge base that would carry me forward over the years and leave me forever linked to the rough-and-tumble past of the original beaver-trapping mountain men.

12

FOX AND COYOTE

Rain was falling in oversized globules that made a dense noise when they hit the ground beside me. As I raised a club over my head, I could feel rainwater pooling at the ends of my bushy eyebrows. Through the blur of that slow and steady rain, I looked down into the eyes of the fox that was now profusely bleeding from his face, and I thought of my daughter. She had an inflatable toy that she loved to play with that looked just like the red fox I was now trying to put out of its misery—a misery which I had caused.

Tucking those thoughts away, I brought the club down hard on the nape of the fox's neck and finished the job.

For quite a while, I sat there petting the wet mats of hair on that animal, while the blood from its mangled face mixed with the pooling rainwater and slowly seeped into the dry fall ground. I had promised myself and my family when I started to hunt and trap that I wouldn't let any animal needlessly suffer, but here I was pushing those boundaries.

I felt guilty, tired, and cold.

A Trapper's Life

The morality of trapping is a funny thing. When I started, I had no idea of the world that I was stepping into. I had first thought of trapping as a way to connect with my past, to build some resilience, and to learn a trade that could provide my family with warm clothes one day if needed, which was all true.

What I did not expect to learn, however, were the deep ties that trapping has to core moral principles and human nature, our economy, and wildlife conservation. I also wasn't expecting it to be so physically and emotionally taxing.

After just a few seasons of running traplines, I am confident that the modern American fur trapper is the hardest working human in our society. Often for low margins, trappers haul by hand hundreds of pounds of equipment into the woods, and to remain within legal and ethical bounds, they check their lines every twenty-four to forty-eight hours, all between the demands of a regular nine-to-five job. Before even entering the woods, trappers spend hours adjusting and perfecting traps to be as humane as possible, which includes welding springs, swivels, and long lengths of chain. It involves precise problem-solving with many variables and moving parts, not unlike solving algorithmic problems in the tech world.

Once an animal gets caught, the first order of business for a trapper is to quickly and painlessly dispatch the animal and get it out of the woods for processing. If a nontarget species is caught, trappers must also play wrangler. Just like Jasper and Horace from *101 Dalmations,* most trappers carry a catch pole to hold a nontarget animal by the neck while they navigate around razor-sharp claws to try and release it from the holding device, putting the caught animal's safety over their own.

As a clear example, one of Idaho's modern-day trapping legends and president of the Idaho Trappers Association, Rusty Kramer, once had to release two mountain lions that were caught in his wolf traps in a single day. Yes, two *mountain lions* released *by hand* all before punching into his day job at 9:00 a.m.

Rusty Kramer of IAT releasing mountain lions.

When a trapper does catch and dispatch his target animal, he has to get it out of the woods and back to his or her home processing facility. Plans for dinner that night? Kiss them goodbye, as there is only a short window of time to skin and board the quarry before rot sets in. Tired and weary, the trapper then has to maintain focus throughout the skinning process, as one small slip of the knife could slice holes in the pelt, which directly affects its profitability at market.

After the pelts are dried and ready for sale, the trapper then has to get them to market, which is not as straightforward as it sounds. Attending trade shows across the region is about the only way to sell enough hides to make it worth the trapper's while.

Even with all that work, factors outside of the trapper's control affect the price of fur on an almost quarterly basis, leaving the trapper guessing as to whether or not the pursuit is even worth it.

Yes, the American trapper is the hardest working individual in America today. But sitting next to the fox I had just deftly bludgeoned with a makeshift club in order to preserve the integrity of its pelt, I had to question my ties to that demanding profession.

I had joined the Idaho Trappers Association around the same time I started beaver trapping. The Tom Miranda book collection that I had bought to kick off that waterborne adventure happened to also contain two books specifically on foothold trapping for predators, both foxes and coyotes. Though I hadn't thought much about that pursuit, my interest snowballed after reading about Tom's techniques, approaches, and justifications for wild canine trapping.

The book specifically touched on the ecological needs for predator control and covered how predator species wreaked havoc on local wildlife and domestic animals across the nation. Tom used a great example of the eastern coyote, an animal I had first seen during my deer hunting back in Tennessee.

I remember my ex-father-in-law would complain about the influx of coyotes in the area. I didn't think much of it at the time, but you could hear them each morning and night howling loudly in the woods. He would tell me how local farmers were begging people to kill them, as they would harass cattle and steal chickens on a daily basis. There would also be nightly news reports of small house dogs or cats being attacked by groups of those predators. They were so abundant that I even had one walk nonchalantly under my tree stand, following a small fawn that had walked by minutes earlier, with the hopes of making it dinner.

Because of those issues, there was an unspoken rule around coyotes in that Tennessee town, and likely the whole Southeast, which was "if you see 'em, shoot 'em.'" At the time, I couldn't really grasp that seemingly wasteful concept. However, moving to the mountains changed my mind.

Getting to see firsthand the impact that canine predators imposed on people making a living off the land, whether in agriculture or self-sustained living, was eye-opening. Idaho Fish and Game would regularly post numbers of cattle killed and data around the growing number of predators expanding throughout the region, which brought about further evidence of a need for control.

After absorbing all of that information, including the instruction from my new trapping books, I decided to try my hand at catching some of these predators on my trapline. My goal was elementary: I wanted to learn to catch, process, and use the furs, while also protecting some of the local domestic and wild game that lived in our region.

Simple, I thought.

However, it turned out that catching a wild dog in the expanse of wilderness where I lived would be much harder than it sounded. To put it in perspective, I was trapping in over three thousand acres of open country, and I would need a wild canine to step directly onto an area of less than half a square foot. And with many rules and regulations around trapping, it was not as easy as setting out bait and waiting for an animal to come to it. You had to study the terrain and the animal's habits to even get close.

Learning the Trapper Trade

Before setting foot in that expanse of wilderness, I first had to purchase and learn the mechanics of a canine foothold trap. Having never been exposed to or coached by anyone about canine trapping, my head immediately went to the cartoon caricature of a trap:

Two jaws with spikes on them that break the leg and hold any animal unfortunate enough to step on it.

That's the "Wile E. Coyote" visual that most Americans probably have when thinking about trapping. It's a visual that couldn't be further from the truth. In reality, modern-day traps are built to hold, not injure, an animal. When used correctly, the animal is trapped above the thick paw pad, which leaves space around the joint for it to move. The animal's pad itself acts as a stopper, preventing it from pulling its foot out of the holding device.

Not knowing which modern-day trapping devices I actually needed, I again visited my favorite Idaho trapping supply store and was coached by some of the amazing ladies who work there. Knowing what I was after, they provided me with many different types and brands of traps and coached me on something I hadn't deeply considered while I had been out beaver trapping: scent control.

Canines are damn smart. Their olfactory receptors can smell much more than humans can, and any bit of human or mechanical scent left on a trap or chain will send them in the opposite direction—a hard lesson I would soon learn.

So, with my new mechanical gadgets in hand, I went to work de-scenting my traps. Each one had to be boiled with some mild soap to remove any factory oil, hung to dry and rust slightly, and then reboiled with natural scents and dye. Afterwards, each trap has to be handled with cotton gloves that are washed with a scent-removing detergent to avoid recontaminating them with human scents.

After a few weeks of prepping the traps, I was forced to get over my fear of actually setting them. As a general rule for life, if you want to know how strong or weak you are, all you need to do is grab even a small foothold trap and try to open it by hand. There's a technique to be used, but opening and setting those traps does take some raw farm-boy strength, something I'd develop over time. It took several attempts, but eventually I was able to open all of my traps without catching myself in them.

Once I had a baseline comfort on using my traps, I decided my first target would be some of the local foxes that we had patrolling the rear of our property. After reading up on the principles of making a dirthole set, which is essentially a trap buried in the dirt, I set out to make my first attempt.

Hiking up a steep ridge where I had frequently seen foxes, I dug my first hole. I placed my live trap in it, put a wire-mesh pan cover over the trigger, and began to shower it with dirt until it was indistinguishable from the ground around it. The chain was anchored to a nearby tree and buried to prevent any animal from seeing it on approach. Before leaving, I placed some fox gland lure nearby to hopefully draw in some of the local populace.

That night I felt terrible anxiety. Not far from my own home and close to our town, I had set a live canine trap, and my mind played out every worst-case scenario. What if our neighbor's dogs were out at night and caught wind of the lure and decided to investigate? What would happen if I caught some other species of animal that I didn't have a permit for?

The unknowns of being a new trapper were paralyzing.

With almost zero sleep that first night, I anxiously made my way the next morning to my first dirt-hole set with my .22-caliber rifle in tow. Excitement initially filled my body as I approached my trap. I could see there was a clear disturbance around the set I had made, but like every new experience I had in the woods up to that point, my ego was quickly and humiliatingly deflated.

When I got closer, I could see that a sly little fox had completely uncovered my trap without setting it off. He had dug around it, pulled it out of its hidey-hole, and even removed the wire-mesh pan cover. To further certify his dominance over me, the fox had peed right on my trap and walked off unharmed. I remade my set and settled in for what would be a long and complicated back-and-forth between myself and my first trapped canine.

That same scenario played out over and over again for the next few weeks. Feeling once again like the movie *Groundhog Day*, I graduated to putting out multiple traps at a time, tried different setups, and became increasingly frustrated at my inability to outwit those animals.

Nightly, I would ask Olesya how such a small animal was so much smarter than me? Every trick I read about in books and viewed on YouTube did not seem to help, but thankfully my wife encouraged me to just stick with it. After nearly a month of daily adjustments and pitched mental battles, I finally connected.

Making my daily trip out to one of my sets, my ears caught the first indication that something was different. I could hear the rattling of chains upon my approach, and my heart began to race as I crested the hill to see a beautiful, large red fox sitting patiently for my arrival.

It surprised me how calm the fox was.

It was as if he knew that the game he had been winning for the last month was now over. I approached within ten feet, raised my rifle to my shoulder, put the crosshairs right between his eyes, and pulled the trigger. His front paws crumpled under his chest, and he was instantaneously dispatched.

As I went to investigate closer, I was relieved to see that this fox did not look as if it had been in pain. Its front paw, which had been caught, was undamaged, an indication that he had not been there long when I arrived. I said a quick prayer of thanks for the fox's sacrifice and made the short walk back to my workshop where I was able to handle and examine my catch.

Skinning a Fox

It turned out that the fox was a *she* with beautiful, thick, red fur and a bushy tail. Her white underbelly was soft and contrasted her pitch-black paws. It was amazing to be up close as I began to brush out her fur to remove any ticks, cockleburs, or other debris.

With my iPad set up beside me, I was about to attempt skinning my first fur-bearing canine, which would require a completely different technique than what I used for squirrels, beavers, and big game. Wearing an oversized plastic apron, I began to follow my virtual YouTube teacher, step by step. I entered my knife just behind the Achilles tendon and ran it all the way down the color change in the fur to the anus. The instructor made it look seamless with one cut that took about two seconds.

I, on the other hand, took nearly five minutes. My blade wouldn't quite set, I kept having to brush fur out of the way, and I couldn't shake the thought of our similarly sized shih tzu, who was sleeping peacefully upstairs. After some struggling, I was able to match the instructor and then replicate the cut again on the other side.

Next it was time to cut off the feet. Going below the elbow, the instructor quickly zipped his knife around and twisted the feet off without breaking any bone. I tried to follow suit but quickly found myself cutting into bone and getting lost in fur once again. I was so focused that when I pulled on one of the tendons, the fox's nails curled inward and scratched up against my forearm and caused me to instinctively jump back. Soon, out of frustration, I just grabbed the paw, twisted it till it broke, and cut off the loose fur.

First attempt at skinning and fleshing a fox.

Not the best first attempt.

I then moved to the portion of instruction that guided me to make intricate cuts around the vent. Just as I heard the instructor say, "Be careful," my knife punctured the anus, letting out a god-awful smell, a stench that would stick with me for the rest of the exercise and be an omnipresent reminder of how inept I was.

Pushing through the stench, I was now able to pull the fur away from the meat on each of the thighs. It peeled away easily and had a crinkling sound as the fat and connective tissue gave way with each pull. That also cleared up the area below the anus at the base of the tail, and using a tool called a tail-stripper, I began removing the tailbone from the surrounding fur. But try as I might, I couldn't quite get the technique of the push-pull motion that the instructor was showing. I sat there wrestling with it for some time, and in another fit of frustration, I finally pulled as hard as I could. The tailbone released itself from the tiny bits of flesh holding it to the fur with a force that caused the bloody tailbone to whack me right in the face.

Taking a calming breath, I giggled, wiped the blood from my cheek, and admired how long the tailbones of those animals were.

The next part of the process was to take a handful of fur and start to pull it down toward the head. It was just like unrolling a sock and went very quickly, only needing a gentle cut through some of the connective tissue. The fur sock made it all the way to the arms before I had to once again consult the video to see how to pull it through.

Using my fingers as probes, I poked through some connective tissue in what would be the armpit of the fox. With some more brute force, I pulled the forearms out and went back to pulling the fur sock toward the head. As I made my way to the base of the neck, the color on the hide changed from a pearl white to a crimson red on the back of the skull. This was an indication that I was coming up to where I had shot her with my .22-caliber rifle.

Unexpectedly, as the hide passed this hole, a slow oozing of brain matter and skull fragments started to sputter out with the pressure that I was applying. Instantaneously, my gag reflexes kicked in. I dry-heaved as the hole oozed like a blood-and-bone-filled pimple.

I had to step outside to collect myself and once again ask myself how badly I wanted this experience. I could drive a few hours to Target and buy clothes off the rack, instead of trapping fur in the wild. Why subject myself to learning this old trade the hard way? Well, I had sought out *real* experiences over digital ones; it just turns out that real experiences often carry painful reminders of just how grim life can be in the natural world. There is no AI-driven filter to cover up the brutality of how we as a species have survived for centuries.

After letting some fresh air reset my brain, I applied an old corporate Jedi mind trick that I use when I find myself in stressful situations at work. I started to box breathe: four Mississippi seconds of sucking air deep into my lungs, four seconds of holding my breath with full lungs, followed by four seconds to slowly push all of that air out of my lungs, and finally four seconds of holding my breath once more without any oxygen. I rinsed and repeated that cycle until my nerves were once again back at baseline and then went back inside my workshop.

With a newly cleared head, I prepared to do the last part, which demanded the most finesse with the blade, cutting the skin around the face. In order to preserve the integrity of the eyes, ears, and nose, I would have to blindly figure out where they were in relation to my blade and figure out how to cut them out. It was a skill I could only learn by trying, and one that I screwed up royally.

Despite my best efforts, that poor fox came out looking like a kid's doll in a horror movie. One ear was nearly "van Goghed," the eye holes looked like a Japanese cartoon character, and I had entirely cut off the snout. It was so bad that I ended up cutting everything off right behind the ears before I went to my newly built fleshing board to finish cleaning up what was left of the hide.

With my brand-new fleshing knife, which resembled an old Soviet scythe, I set about cleaning off the residual fat from the hide, just like the instructor was showing me on YouTube. Trying to mimic his technique as best I could, I let the dull side of my blade run down the exposed flesh of the fox, but with horror, I watched as my very first stroke ripped a quarter size hole in the pelt.

After some self-berating, I slowly began to get the hang of it as small reams of fat began to collect on the floor around me. Once that was done, I washed the fur in some warm water and dish soap before placing it on a specialized board to dry, then took my homework upstairs to show my wife.

God bless her reaction as she told me how beautiful it was, despite the gaping holes and the lack of a face. She knew how much time I had put into the craft and was proud of me either way. It was welcome encouragement, seeing that it had taken me over three hours to skin and board one fox.

My resolve wasn't completely extinguished, though, as I knew that I would have more traps to check and more chances to perfect my own technique in hopes of eventually having furs worthy to sell and use for clothing.

It wasn't until year two, however, after spending the summer scouting perfect trapping locations on our long family hikes, that I was able to connect more consistently. I did more research on traplines and started to set them longer. This allowed me to trap more animals, which gave me more experience skinning with the knife.

Trapping Coyotes

It was in my second season that I began trapping coyotes. Similar to foxes, these canines were abundant in my area, as they had not been pursued in earnest by hunters or trappers in the last decade. The sets and techniques used for coyotes were nearly identical to what I used for foxes, and as my lines spread out across more open country, I had about as equal a chance of catching a fox in my foothold traps as I did a coyote.

Second-season fox.

The main difference between the trapped fox and coyote, however, was the fur yield and price you could receive at market. Of all of the furs, coyote happened to be doing the best, with very interested buyers from China paying up to ninety dollars per pelt for prime western coyote fur. The first time I intentionally set a coyote line and caught one, it was a very different experience than catching a fox. In the same vein, I could hear the chains rattle as I got closer to my traps, but the violence in which they shook was palpably different.

As the size of the canines I trapped increased, so did the kinetic violence that could be felt in the aura that these dogs gave off as you approached them. Despite following the same dispatching method I had gotten used to at that point, a .22 rifle shot, the hair on my arms raised much higher than with the fox I had dealt with prior. Every time I approached one of these aggressive and trapped animals, my guts would contort just a little bit until my fight-or-flight reaction was subdued by the knowledge that the chained threat was ethically neutralized.

The Trapping Community

My furs started to become less grotesque and more eligible for retail purchase during my second season, which forced me to start attending fur-buying conventions. At those events, I began to learn more about who actually purchases the pelts that trappers work so hard to get.

What I hadn't realized was that there were tons of luxury brands that prefer to use real fur due to its durability, renewability, and warmth. Brands such as Canada Goose, Balenciaga, Louis

Vuitton, Marc Jacobs, Dior, and Yves Saint Laurent still used real fur for their high-end products.

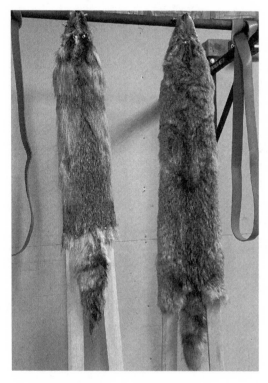

Beautiful cross fox and coyote.

During all those years I spent working as a drone in Manhattan, Washington, DC, and San Francisco, I would see person after person wearing beautiful, black Canada Goose jackets with coyote-fur-lined hoods. As I look back on that time, it's funny to think that I had no idea that behind each one of those designer jackets was a trapper. Each fur-lined hood meant someone had spent cold, early mornings trapping those animals, and even more time delicately skinning and delivering the perfect pelt to market.

Attending those conventions also allowed other community members to evaluate my pelts and give me feedback on how to get top grades in order to serve some of those high-end retailers. They gently pointed out to me that my pelts each had small holes near the face where I would dispatch the animals with my .22 rifle. In a good faith suggestion, one fur-grader suggested that I could avoid that issue by dispatching the animals in a different, albeit more personal way: clubbing them.

I was slightly taken aback, but he assured me that this was humane and pointed me to a wonderful online documentary called *Trapper Jake*, which followed an old-timer around his traplines. To preserve the integrity of his pelts, Jake would take a metal pipe, quickly walk up to his catch, and hit them on the head, killing them in one painless swing. Having done that thousands of times, if not hundreds of thousands, his accuracy and swiftness were admirable, and the process did, in fact, seem to be efficient and humane.

After absorbing the documentary, that method of dispatch found a comfortable home in the recesses of my brain. It was only after a long, rainy drive home from a trapping convention in Boise that it emerged in an actionable way. Tired from the four-hour drive back to my cabin, I found myself in a position where I still needed to go check my traplines, which I had no desire to do with the increasing rain outside.

Moral Dilemma

Overcoming my laziness and self-pity, I loaded up our side-by-side vehicle with my trapping equipment and dispatching rifle and made my way to my first set. When I neared the hill where my traps were set, I pulled out my binoculars and realized that I had a red fox in my first trap. I pulled up closer to prepare myself to do what I had now done dozens of times.

However, as I stepped out of the utility vehicle, I caught sight of a forearm-sized log that reminded me of the club that Trapper Jake had used to dispatch his animals. By reflex and without forethought, I left my rifle in the UTV, picked up the log, and made my way to the patiently waiting fox.

As the rain began to drench my neck and I sat there staring at the fox, I did some mental judo to convince myself to take the same action I had seen Trapper Jake take in the video. With an awkward movement that married a baseball and golf swing, I lifted my natural mace and brought it down where I assumed I should: right on top of the fox's head.

With that death strike, I tore a hole in my quarry's face, and blood splattered my wet boots. My mind reeled then with a sudden existential crisis, thinking about my daughter and her stuffed fox toy, my own morality, and the desire for commercial perfection that led me to bludgeon the fox instead of shooting it.

The tears that welled in my eyes were the first that I had openly shed since my divorce. They were triggered by the sudden violence of the action, and connected most deeply to the innermost feelings of an exhausted hunter out fending for his family and needing to painlessly dispatch a beautiful creature, a fellow traveler on this Earth. The act of crushing that fox's skull with a club felt more violent and inhumane to me than a single bullet to the head.

I took my catch home and discussed the experience with my wife, who then became upset at me because my standard operating procedure was to cover up my emotions with humor about the event. Olesya felt that I had not taken the bludgeoning seriously. It wasn't until the next day that I found the maturity to discuss with her what I had actually felt during the experience.

Once we cleared the air between us, I set about skinning the fox. It was one that I would tan but not sell. I knew that fox would stay with me forever, both physically and mentally, and be a constant reminder to be true to myself and my morals. What I'd learned was that a painless death via a .22-caliber bullet was more valuable to me than a completely holeless pelt to be used by some distant luxury goods designer.

13

WOLF

The hair on the back of my neck stood on end as I heard the howl roll down from the hillside above me. In response, I let out my best reciprocation and started a conversation with one of the most beautiful and violent animals on earth, the gray wolf.

As I waited between howls, my eyes locked on to the ponderosa pines surrounding me, and my mind began to melt into my past. I was no longer sitting deep in the woods but transported back to childhood where I was sitting in my grandfather's little cabin in north Georgia, staring at a wood-framed painting of a wolf.

I wasn't exactly close with my grandfather, and by the time I was eight or nine, he was chronically sick with issues ranging from cancer to diabetes and everything in between. My grandfather and I never sat and had deep conversations or interacted much outside of holidays, but I loved that cabin, the rustic life he seemed to live, and that wolf painting.

Wherever I went in that small cabin, the eyes of that framed wolf would follow me as if it were watching my every move. Its gravity would pull me in and transport me to different worlds where I was the main character in my own mountain-man play. I spent a lot of my youth in that mind state of wanderlust, under the watchful eye of that wolf.

When my grandfather eventually passed away, there wasn't much to go around, but the one thing I received as a legacy of his bloodline was the wolf painting. It went with me everywhere I lived. I brought it to college, where I had to fight to get it back from an ex-girlfriend's house, then to my overseas jobs after college, where I valued its safekeeping and safety more than my own. Through all of that painting's travels, it had now found a home in my own little, wooden cabin in central Idaho, similar to my grandfather's cabin where it had started its journey.

Spirit Animal

As I continued to mentally soar through my own personal history, another howl from a not-so-distant wolf brought me back to reality, just as the psilocybin began to wear off. You see, I wasn't out hunting on that wolf-filled trip. Instead, I was on a vision quest to look inward and try to understand who I had become. I also wanted to know who I wanted to be in the future. I was just lucky enough to find myself interacting with my spirit animal out in the wild.

Wolf was the animal that had solidified my choice to move to Idaho just a few years before. It was also the animal I had heard most about since moving to Idaho. People in both the hunting and nonhunting communities loved to talk about wolves, their reintroduction to the wild, and how they should be managed. In fact, it was close to impossible to find a more divisive topic in the state.

One side was fully entrenched in the camp of letting the now thousands of wolves run free, and to protect them as an endangered species. The other side, which was composed mostly of ranchers and hunters, believed the reintroduction of wolves negatively affected their abilities to keep strong numbers in both domestic herds of cattle and wild herds of deer and elk.

When I started to explore and learn about wolf hunting and trapping in Idaho, I knew I was bound to get ensnared in my own moral dilemma, as I truly believed that I had a deep spiritual connection with wolves. So instead of setting out right away to hunt and trap wolves just for the sake of it, I decided to take my time and do some research during my first year in Idaho. I started by reaching out to biologists and commissioners at Idaho Fish and Game, and spoke with people both for and against the practice of culling wolves.

With all of the information I was pulling in, I was able to see both sides of the issue extremely clearly.

On one hand, I loved these animals. They had been a central theme in my life since I was a young boy at my grandfather's cabin. I would sit in his leather chair and stare at that wolf painting while reading *Call of the Wild* and dreaming of befriending and taming my own wolf one day. Those dreams as a boy, however, were naive, with no concept of what it was like to interact with wolves in their natural and violence-prone environment.

The tipping point of my relationship with wolves was when I was regularly and graphically exposed to the impacts they have on the areas where they have been reintroduced. For example, in our small Idaho village alone, we have five recorded packs of varying size roaming around at any given time. We could often hear them howling in the late evenings as we sat on our front porch and were left wondering what game they were chasing and about to kill.

The evidence of those orchestrated and murderous howls was usually found quite easily the next day, as buzzards, crows, and bald eagles would start circling the air over the remnants of wolf kills. In our region, it was rare in the winter to drive down our long dirt road and not come up on multiple kills. Sometimes, if we were lucky and driving early in the morning or late evening, we would catch the glimpse of multiple sets of eyes in the pines, circling not too far from their kills. The power that those canines possess is otherworldly, and the brutal murder scenes they left behind were impressively gory.

As I began to speak with more hunters and trappers about the wolf issue in Idaho, I would hear stories that often seemed unbelievable. There were credible accounts of wolves busting or chewing through heavy-duty chains and traps, wolves walking off with injuries from large-caliber rifles, and wolves surrounding and attacking hunters who happened to accidentally stumble upon a den.

Those accounts were numerous enough to warrant some deep thought on a few different aspects of the reality I now lived in. For one thing, I was out hunting and hiking in those wolf-occupied lands with my family and personal pets. Two, I was seeing the physical evidence of the rate at which they kill elk and deer in my region, which was estimated to be around 2.2 elk per wolf every thirty days.

For me, the straw that broke the camel's back in my decision to pursue wolves was an experience during my second season of archery elk hunting. After a few glorious days engaging bugling bulls, we were greeted one morning by the sounds of wolves howling around our camp. The next two days, in the middle of the rut, we would see elk in the distance, but not a single one would bugle. The presence and overabundance of wolves was actually changing the way elk and deer vocalized and interacted with each other in those wild places.

Wolf Trapping

Armed with enough information to make my decision, I set out to get closer to wolves, understand them better, and eventually try to harvest one. No longer would my encounters be just by chance or luck. I was going to kill my spirit animal and by extension, kill the last remnants of my former naive self in the process.

Idaho, despite preconceived notions, was actually quite strict on licensure for hunting and trapping wolves. Yes, if you are a licensed hunter, you can buy several over-the-counter tags for hunting wolves, but very few of those are actually filled.

Most hunters purchase those tags to keep in their wallets *just in case* they run into wolves while hunting other species. To drive home how difficult wolves are to hunt and trap, in 2019, more than forty-five thousand Idaho wolf tags were sold to the public. Of those, only 188 wolves were taken statewide, with the majority of those killed by seasoned trappers. Furthermore, to actually trap wolves, there was an extra course that was mandated by Idaho Fish and Game.

After having made my decision to pursue wolves in earnest, I was able to sign up for one of the few wolf-trapping courses offered before the COVID pandemic sent everything into lockdown. The course was taught by Fish and Game officers, biologists, and some of the state's leading wolf trappers.

Over the course of eight hours, I learned more about wolves, foothold trapping, snaring, and general woodsmanship than I had been able to in my fumbling around in the woods by myself for the year prior. I walked away from that course realizing that even the best-trained wolf trappers and hunters struggled to capture those elusive animals, as wolves typically run huge swaths of land over about a thirty-day period. Meaning if there was a fresh wolf kill, it was likely the pack that consumed that animal wouldn't be back in that area for almost a month. So, if you set traps around that kill at the legally preordained distance (at least thirty feet), it was very likely that your traps would go untouched for weeks on end.

That equates to an increased chance that heavy snows or precipitation would wash away or cover your traps and render them less effective. It also increased the chances of getting a nontarget catch, meaning you would have to spend more money and time to get out in the woods to check those traps regularly.

Though daunting, I set out that year to get some trapping steel on the ground and get in the game. I let the people in my town know what I was up to, and to be on the lookout for fresh wolf kills or roadkill in and out of town. At the same time, I was constantly scouting for birds circling above the trees around town that might point me toward a fresh kill.

It was weeks before I was finally alerted to a freshly killed elk calf outside of town. I threw on my scentless white cotton gloves, loaded my traps into a scent-free box, and rushed to the grotesque scene. I pulled up on the side of a snow-covered dirt road where I found a small eviscerated elk calf. It was only recognizable by its face and remaining ribs, which loosely held up pieces of hide dangling like fashionable fringe over the large opening in its empty internal cavity.

The snow around it had a pinkish hue that faded back to white snow in the direction the wolves had clearly left. As per law, I could not move the carcass and could not set any traps within thirty feet of the animal or the public roadway. So I set out to study the terrain and tracks of those wolves to make an educated guess as to how they may come back to revisit the carcass.

Improvising by replicating sets that had worked for foxes and coyotes, I started laying out my traps. Most were trail sets, which are positioned directly on a trail a wolf repeatedly travels in its territory. The traps are designed to catch a wolf by one of its paws. I anchored some to trees, and others to downed timber to act as drags.

Satisfied with my work, I went home for a sleepless night, during which my mind raced. I kept second-guessing myself about whether or not my sets were optimal and wondering if there was something caught in them.

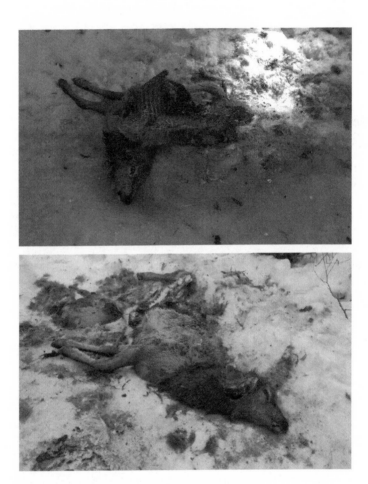

A couple of winter wolf kills.

I knew I had a window of about thirty days before the wolf pack moved on from that area. So I dedicated myself to making something happen in that limited timeframe.

Wolf dirt-hole set near a natural kill site.

For twenty-six days, I would wake up, head out, and check my traps from a distance, but each day I was disappointed. Some days I would even find other kills further and further away from where my traps were set. It shook my resolve and made me consider pulling my existing traps and moving them to the new kill.

On day twenty-seven, after setting my first wolf traplines, I decided to pull them out and try something new. When I looked back at the trail camera that I had set up, I was delighted to see that I'd had several visitors—foxes, coyotes, and mountain lions— but nothing heavy enough to fire off my wolf traps.

For the rest of that season, I moved my traps over and over again for long, patient periods around both natural and road kills. I was never able to connect and never actually got eyes on any wolves, but I did see plenty of signs. It was as if the wolves had a sixth sense for me, and would go up and investigate each and every trap just to let me know they were there and that they were smarter than I was. There would be huge paw prints right up to my traps, before they took a hard ninety-degree turn and went around them. It was like two butt ends of magnets pushing against each other whenever they got close.

Two old-timer's collection of wolf pelts.

Wolves humbled me in my first season of hunting them, and continue to humble me to this day. As I sit writing this book, I still have yet to find a way to capture and kill my spirit animal. I have continued to make mistakes, catch myself in traps, and have come oh so close to getting one several times. Wolves are a species that I have invested hundreds of days pursuing, yet I feel like I know less now about wolf hunting and trapping than I did when I started. It's the perfect parallel to my own spiritual journey and evolution, both of which I will continue to work on for the rest of my earthly life.

PART IV

TWENTY FIRST CENTURY MOUNTAIN MAN

Whenever we go to the mountains, we find more than we seek.

—JOHN MUIR

14

WELCOME TO WHOVILLE

The sound of the underbelly of our car getting ripped out was unmistakable. As soon as I heard the first crunching sound and felt the car lurch hard to the right, I knew we were in trouble. I had not seen the rock hiding in the snow, as Olesya and I, our seven-month-old daughter, and our two dogs were making our way to Boise for our extended-family Thanksgiving celebration.

When we made contact with the rock, my brain immediately started to convince me that there was nothing wrong and that our car would handle the impact just fine. It was 5:30 a.m., five degrees Fahrenheit, and we were fifteen miles from our town when the car shut off and rolled to a stop.

Smack dab in the middle of the snow-covered dirt road under a canopy of pines, we sat helpless before I grabbed my headlamp to get out and survey the damage. That rock had split our skid plate, punctured our transmission pan, and left dents and holes down the rest of the car's underside before pinching the muffler shut in its final act of hatred. Looking at the road behind us, I could see a distinct trail of transmission fluid leading four hundred yards back to the impact site.

Freezing, I got back into the car.

Knowing that most of our town would be asleep, I pulled out my Garmin GPS device and started to fire off a few messages to different folks. With no cell phone service, I would have to hope that one of our friends had their internet on and would hear their phone vibrate.

After ten minutes with no answers, I began to think critically of what I would have to do next. If no one answered, I would have to bundle up my wife and infant in the back of the car with the extra blankets we always carry, and then make the long and cold fifteen-mile walk back to our house to get our second vehicle. That would take hours, and I worried about their ability to stay warm for that long.

Racking my brain, I remembered that one of the couples who lived in town with us was on vacation in the Bahamas. I sent a satellite message to them in hopes they were up and able to make a direct call to our fire chief's landline. After a few minutes of anxious waiting, I got a message back saying that our fire chief was on his way and would be out to us in the next few hours. Saving me the cold walk, we were able to sit together as a family in the cold predawn morning and think about how lucky we were to have found ourselves ingrained in the local community we were now part of.

Home Sweet Home

Part of the reason we found ourselves living in that town, at the end of a long dirt road to nowhere, was because I had always been easily seduced by the impossible. If something was hard to attain or had low odds of success, I was usually the first to sign up. I liked testing and understanding my limits, which held true for when I first left Louisiana and made my way westward. After having that confirming spiritual interaction with the lone crow under the shadows of Arches National Park, I had been determined to go into the woods, learn to hunt and trap, and come out from an altogether solo journey a rougher and tougher individual. As such, when I moved to our new little town, I felt more comfortable initially observing the people in my self-imposed experiment from a distance.

Considered a village within our large Idaho county, the reality was that our "town" was just a forgotten speck on the edge of a wilderness map. We paid taxes for amenities that we did not have access to, such as public education, public power, and law enforcement, yet whenever we would send representation to our county's public meetings, our complaints and requests were most often answered with a scoff or muted laugh.

Our little village was, by necessity, self-sufficient in terms of utilities, amenities, and self-governance. To provide for that small group of pioneers, over the years there was a dam built on the river to draw hydroelectricity. Town water was sourced and cleaned through a co-op, we kept a small volunteer fire and EMS staff, and we ran a rural highway department that was all handled by a year-round population of thirty-eight people. Every one of those full-time residents put out a *lot* of effort to help keep those basic amenities up and running, especially considering that most of the tools and equipment used to service everything would look perfectly at home in some bougie ski-town antique shop.

To add to this, Mother Nature didn't seem to care about anyone's creature comforts. The combination of old equipment and manic weather would usually manifest itself in frequent power outages, occasional low water pressure, wildfire danger, and blocked passage on our roadways due to downed trees, rockslides, or avalanches. Though that may all sound like anarchy, there were unwritten but known rules that everyone seemed to adhere to, which made everything work.

Our town's two-man road crew clearing trees after a spring storm.

Learning those rules as a new outsider and getting involved with the heartbeat of the town was not easy at first. I found out there was a vetting process. To put it lightly, when I first moved in, I was met with suspicion. I was a young, divorced guy from out of state who did not like to socialize. I would sit up in my cabin, working away on my hunting and trapping pursuits in between toiling away online at my remote tech job to make ends meet, and rarely made public appearances.

It was not until I met Olesya (by the grace of God) that I started to get pulled out of my self-made shell and to realize that the community I was living in was not only special but necessary. Olesya would joke with me that I was like the Grinch sitting up in my cabin, looking down on Whoville with a curmudgeonly attitude, only sliding down on large holidays to get into some mischief before retreating back to my lair. But like the Grinch, my small, beat-up heart would eventually grow three sizes by interacting with and getting to know my neighbors. Ultimately, it would help heal the pain I had been through in my divorce and sweeten the already wonderful experiences I was having in the woods.

That gradual chipping away of my exterior defenses started by slowly opening a dialogue with our town fire chief, a gruff lifelong fireman from the DC area who moved out to the end of the road to dredge for gold and never went back. Over the years, he had built up a local volunteer crew that was surprisingly well trained for fire, search and rescue, and EMS.

Tactically, he slowly eroded my defenses, and with a nudge from my new wife, he got me to start attending some training sessions that he was hosting. In those training sessions, I began to realize that the entire year-round population was active in those exercises, including folks who were well into their eighties and still wanted to pull their weight for the town.

Generally, we would have town training every other Wednesday night. We would practice fundamentals of knot tying, CPR, using our VHF radios, and how to coordinate bringing in a Life Flight helicopter. The more intricate lessons ranged from learning to operate the old Vietnam-era fire trucks and ambulances to getting certified to use our own personal equipment in search-and-rescue missions.

Aside from being well trained for any event, the small town was also surprisingly diverse. We had both sides of the political aisle represented, folks who embraced nonlinear sexual orientation, and people of varying degrees of wealth. Whereas those things may matter in bigger cities, this town frankly did not seem to care. What mattered to everyone in our village was that as a community member, you were capable of showing up and helping out when the time came.

And those times would come.

Being nestled at the southern base of the Sawtooth Wilderness meant that during the summer, our campgrounds began to swell with recreaters of all types. People from the greater Boise area would use the space to get away on weekends and often brought their mechanical toys with them. People would rip around on side-by-sides, dirt bikes, and four-wheelers, while others sought fish at some of our high alpine lakes or looked for refuge in the town hot springs and river. No matter the activity, it would inevitably seem to include copious amounts of alcohol.

Visitors to our region generally knew that there was no law enforcement to deal with, and they took that to heart. Without fail, we would get weekly EMS calls to campgrounds for things ranging from heatstroke, broken bones, and fights to puncture wounds, lacerations, and everything in between.

Occasionally there would be fatalities. Over the years they hadn't been frequent, usually small plane crashes, but my first fatal encounter was from an alcohol-related ATV incident.

First Responders

One midsummer evening after putting our newborn down to sleep, my wife and I were sitting down for dinner. As we took our first bites of food, the VHF radio we kept in the kitchen started to go off, and I could immediately hear the panic in the voice on the other end. There was a request for any EMS or fire personnel to get to specific coordinates, quickly. I grabbed my gear bag, kissed my wife, and left my plate of food untouched. I didn't know it at the time, but I wouldn't be home until the next day.

When I arrived on the scene a short time later, it was pure madness. There was a flipped ATV and multiple wounded people. Through the zombie-like bodies, I could see one of our fire personnel performing CPR on a large gentleman on the loose-gravel road into our town. I cut through the sea of onlookers to ask what was needed and was instructed to go and get the helipad ready for Life Flight.

As the sun began to set, our small team was able to get the main victim into the back of our ambulance and down to the helipad, where we waited on the Life Flight chopper to arrive. When the ambulance got to the helipad, and we began the long thirty-minute wait for help, I hopped into the rotation of three guys doing aggressive CPR.

What I quickly realized as my turn came around was that the man was already dead, yet we were required to keep up our CPR practice until the chopper arrived. As we continued to rotate doing thirty chest compressions to every failed breath, the sounds of cracking rib cartilage would be intermittently disrupted by the sound of the man's vocal, drunk, and grieving father banging on the ambulance door in despair.

When the EMS flight crew did finally arrive, they were able to quickly pronounce the man as deceased. They ended up taking one of the other injured parties, who was bleeding from his ears and severely concussed, to the hospital.

That departing helicopter kicked off a long and painful night as we drove the now-deceased man and his family back to our small fire station, where we would be waiting five hours for both the coroner and the sheriff to arrive.

It turned out that the family was celebrating the deceased's brother's birthday. He was a new father, had a new job, and was starting a new chapter of life in his early thirties. With his dad, brother, and friends, they decided to drink and have fun on some of the small ATVs they had brought with them.

With no helmets, they were out riding with two people per ATV at max speeds. The gentleman who passed was over three hundred pounds, and his passenger was at least two hundred—well over the weight limit for the ATV, which they managed to flip over, going more than forty miles per hour.

That death, though completely avoidable, showed me the beauty and resilience of our small community. Everyone was there to help console the grieving family, and every person waited until the coroner and sheriff (who both got lost) arrived hours later, before heading home to their own beds.

Those kinds of experiences in tragedy cement a bond that carries over to all aspects of life, including the fun side. As a community, we all celebrate major holidays together as a large pseudofamily. At the one operating bar in town, we do get-togethers for the Fourth of July, Friendsgiving in November, and round out both Christmas and New Year's with large potluck dinners.

That small group of thirty-eight people at the end of the road also know how to party hard. Booze-fueled karaoke nights are a sight to behold, and the amount of talent that permeates such a small group of tightly knit people is impressive. We have professionally trained singers, ex-ballerinas, professional athletes, NASA engineers, and other random talents you would never expect.

Aside from training, joint sorrow, and fun, the whole communal experiment also affords a lot of shared knowledge in general sustainability and independent living, if we bother to ask. It was knowledge that would be vital to our survival as our second full year of living out in the woods kicked off. Because unbeknownst to my wife and me, we were about to get our first full-course tasting in the difficulties of maintaining a remote life in winter wilds.

In anticipation of our second winter, we had decided to build a woodshed that could hold as many as six cords of firewood to help heat our home. I had envisioned a structure that would keep our wood dry and out of the elements and serve as a better option than what we'd had during our first winter—some tarps haphazardly thrown over our frustratingly moist logs.

To help build my shed, I employed the help of my father, who came up from South Carolina. We spent several days building the heavy frame of the woodshed with locally hewn wood, before finishing it off with a tin roof that would hopefully handle the winter snow load with no problem.

Satisfied with our work, I then set about falling, cutting, and splitting wood during the short summer months until the shed was completely full. We felt ready for whatever winter might throw our way.

But winter had different plans for us.

Survival Is Communal

At first, our structure was doing its job perfectly, protecting our valued heat source from the wet snow and allowing us easy access. But once winter started, it never took its foot off the gas, and we went from one foot of snow to over five in the span of a week.

On one of the mornings of our heaviest snowfall, I went to fetch some logs for both of our woodburning stoves, only to find that our woodshed was not visible. Considering it was still dark out, I grabbed a headlamp to try and shed some literal light on the situation, which revealed a laughable scene.

The woodshed we had carefully engineered with a nine-foot-tall front was completely buried in snow and had moved almost a foot from its foundation. It turned out that snow had slid from our roof, and the weight and velocity had so much force that snow was jammed between each and every log, three rows deep.

Without any other option, I changed my early morning work plans and grabbed a shovel. I dug for a few hours before sunlight came up, and my nearest neighbor came to join me. Between shovels, a pickaxe, and a snowblower, we were able to clear a small entry to one portion of the shed to once again gain access to our precious fuel.

A seemingly benign design decision that we had made in the dryness of summer had cost us hours of unforeseen work in subzero winter temperatures. Consequences for actions.

Plans made in summer don't always hold up in winter.

Despite the loner visions that led me to this place, I found myself being continually lifted up and supported by the community of strangers who were all going through the same difficult things on a daily basis. I found that each and every one of the people in our village genuinely cared about the well-being of my family and me. Need help with your snowmobile? Want a sourdough bread starter? Missing a specific tool? Need electrical help? No matter the problem, someone in town would selflessly help solve it.

The humbling nature of those experiences brought me to the hard realization that I could not do everything alone. I was not the lone wolf that I liked to believe I was—a vision that had been cultivated by the ease and convenience of my former life. Yet, out in the "real" world away from supermarkets and stores, the survival of my family, including the freedom to hunt and trap as I wanted to, was truly a communal effort. An effort that required investment of both time and the willingness to help others. It's a byproduct of my Western experiment that I am immensely proud of, and one that helped mold the evolution of my spirit that I would soon come to recognize.

15

JEKYLL AND HYDE

The static of the VHF radio cut me off mid-sentence during a monthly business review with my corporate overlords via Zoom. Trained to listen to the traffic coming from our county dispatch, I quickly muted my work laptop microphone and held a finger up to my camera to indicate that I needed a minute.

"Any available search-and-rescue units, please respond to a distressed hunter at the following coordinates..."

As the dispatcher rattled off some numbers, I fumbled to write them down, and as the only search-and-rescue personnel in town that day, I knew I would have to respond. Turning my mute button back off, I let my bosses know that I would be gone for an unknown amount of time but would make up any lost work once I was back. Before giving them time to respond, I hung up and heard the now universally known "bloop" of a Zoom call ending.

Embracing the dichotomy of my situation, I quickly switched mental gears from day job to woodsman, a feat that had become commonplace over the past few years of living and working remotely in the backcountry. I pulled up a map of the last known response from the distressed hunter, which was a steep five-mile hike from our town. After a quick change of clothes, I grabbed my equipment go-bag, and went to pick up one of our town EMTs who would be joining me.

Hunter in Distress?

It was a hot August day, and this hunter had been out trying to fill an early-season mule deer tag around one of our steep alpine lakes. Apparently he had harvested a deer the day prior, and while processing the animal, he had become dehydrated. He messaged his wife and father back in his home state of Washington that he was sick and puking. They didn't hear anything back for over twelve hours, and fearing the worst, they called the sheriff's office. It was the sheriff's office that put the staticky VHF radio call through to me.

As I made my way to the trailhead, I was able to find his truck and confirmed his license plate with our dispatcher over the radio. In the process, I noticed a spread of Little Debbie snack cakes on the dash of his car. The first morbid thought that ran through my head was *I hope he's not fat because it's going to suck dragging him out of there.* I took a swig of water in the early morning heat and set out toward his coordinates at a jog.

With my bag in tow, it took about an hour and a half to start closing in on the hunter's last known location. As the elevation started to rise more steeply, I caught a glimpse of someone walking down the trailhead in front of me. It was a young, fit guy who had a beautiful velvet-covered mule deer strapped to his back.

He looked strained but confident.

Stopping him, I relayed the information I had from our dispatcher and asked if he had come across a sick, and potentially passed out, hunter further up the trail. With a confused look, he said no and went on his way.

We both walked beyond each other by about one hundred yards before we both doubled back like we were in some sort of romantic comedy. Somehow, intuitively, we both realized we were looking for each other. I shouted back his name, which I had received from dispatch, and he responded with a jovial, "Ya, that's me!"

Relieved that he wasn't fat or dead, I walked back to chat with him.

It turned out that he had been severely dehydrated the day before when he messaged his wife and father. He ended up chugging a lot of water and salt pills to come back from the brink and passed out in his tent to let his body recover. What he had failed to do, however, was turn off his Garmin emergency device, which promptly died while he was asleep. With no way to communicate to his family that he was okay, they assumed the worst.

After some profuse apologies for making us come all the way out to find him, I had him sign a release form and complimented his beautiful deer. Then I started a jog back to the trailhead so I could rejoin the rest of my afternoon work meetings, all while praying that my unexpected and lengthy absence wouldn't lead to me getting fired from my day job.

My Double Life

Concern over losing my day job was something that I had heavily considered when I decided to move out to the woods to pursue my hunting and trapping dreams. I knew my move always carried the potential to negatively impact my career. From the second I left the comfort of asphalt streets, I'd made a point to work with my corporate team to ensure that I would continue to be as available as possible, but I'd made it clear that there could be times when my situation wouldn't allow me to be as ever-present as I had been in the past.

I had to do my best to explain to colleagues the complexities and unknowns that could and would crop up each and every day that may require flexibility for me to handle them. Power outage? Search-and-rescue call? Downed animal? Broken-down vehicles? They were all on the table, and I never knew when they may hit. That negotiated peace I kept with my employer felt like I was walking on eggshells for the first year or so of our experiment.

Every dropped Zoom call from my poor internet connection would initially bring me stomach pain, and when the power would go out, I would be left with no way to communicate to my teammates as to what was going on or where I had gone, since we lacked cellular reception.

The frequency of those interruptions started to wear me down, and I believed that at any minute, I would be fired from the career I had worked so hard to build. I dreaded losing my only source of income that was supporting our whole adventure.

But as time went on, there were no indications that they were reconsidering our work arrangement.

For every Zoom call that I dropped, every extended power outage, every animal that needed to be skinned, and every town emergency that needed response, no one at work complained. It took months of those interactions for me to realize that I was just not that damn important at the company, and not really missed during those short, erratic intervals.

It hurt a little at first, and I started to take stock of the way I had approached work for the past decade. My measure of success before moving to the backcountry had always been the number of plane rides and cities that I traveled to in any given month. Once COVID hit, my value driver had switched to how many meetings I had jammed into my calendar on a given day.

It was a gross realization for me that my entire identity up to that point had been completely wrapped up in my professional career and that veneer of success. And if it weren't for the constraints of our community utilities and the woodsman way of life I was now living, I would still be stuck in that same rut and pattern to this day.

But as time wore on, juggling work in the woods, I began to realize how clearly wrong I had been in approaching my work–life balance. Though I had begun to leave behind the corporate straitjacket I used to wear on a daily basis, I found that I still clung to pieces of my core corporate identity and was reluctant to let them go.

It was only after being continually exposed to my corporate expendability that I realized that before all else, I was now a woodsman, just one that happened to also still make a living at a large corporation. Once I made that personal realization, I was able to start enjoying the unexpected time off, and the anxiety I felt evaporated and faded into the ether. In fact, I started to focus on repackaging all of the calls that had previously littered my calendar into more succinct emails and Slack messages, all of which could be tackled in a more asynchronous manner. I no longer felt that I had to try to be there in real time.

Like magic, meetings started to fall off my calendar like autumn leaves, and I was no longer a slave to my own conjured idea of what I thought success looked like in my field. What's even more ironic is that when I started to let go and embrace my hunter-and-trapper lifestyle, I began finding *more* success in my professional career. The time I spent on work-related tasks became more focused and deliberate, as I knew my day could be derailed at any moment.

That realization also opened me up for even more experiences in the woods, which was the whole reason I was living out there. I no longer worried about the timing or potential impact of checking my traplines early in the morning before work. If there was nothing there, great, but if I had to deal with any number of critters or sketchy situations, I wasn't going to fret about missing a few meetings.

The new work dynamic I was beginning to actually live out was freeing, and I found myself better able to switch between a frontiersman and businessman. Oftentimes in the mornings, I would be skinning an animal, covered in blood, and then stop right in the middle to go to my laptop for a meeting or to craft an email. That daily and visceral connection to life, death, and Earth gave me better perspective and the ability to separate the wheat from the chaff on critical business decisions, getting to the core problems that needed to be addressed more quickly.

My entire lifestyle change also became a bit of a work shtick in and of itself. Depending on the audience, I would be sitting in my workshop with animals in different states of undress in the background behind me. My colleagues and vendor acquaintances became curious about what, where, and why I was living that way. Most calls would start off with a volley of interrogative questions from people with an underpinning of genuine curiosity.

The realization that many others wished for my current life-style was becoming more and more apparent. I was constantly bombarded with the "I'm so jealous," or the "I wish my circum-stances could allow that" comments.

My work email inbox started to pile up with men and women asking me, "How did you get to where you are?" "How do you handle the internet?" "How do you juggle work meetings?" and most frequently, "How did you learn to hunt?"

I could feel the palpable shift in the majority of people I talked with, who were starting to be confronted with the same existen-tial crisis that I had gone through just a few years prior. They seemed to be asking themselves, as I had: "If I needed to, could I survive and provide for my family without fully relying on modern-day infrastructure?"

The COVID pandemic had also planted a seed of doubt and was accentuated by many nationwide failures of infrastructure. People were starting to realize that dependency on govern-ment-run systems could be a dangerous comfort to settle into.

For me, the challenge to learn how to survive was best served by removing myself and my family from that dependency in a sharp and drastic way. I ripped away the bandage of my former identity and replaced it with confidence that only came from learning the basics of human needs and survival: hunting, trapping, garden-ing, community, and basic woodsmanship.

Yet it wasn't lost on me that I was still dependent on my corporate career for money to support my new lifestyle. Our pioneer excursion wouldn't have been possible without my job helping to build cutting-edge technology, so finding the right balance between work and an off-grid lifestyle was key for me, and without balance, I wouldn't have been able to operate.

In fact, I'd found that to give my all at my job in more efficient ways, I actually *needed* to live in the backcountry. To give my all meant that when I disconnected from work, I needed to hear silence, to have no cell service, and to truly be unplugged. I knew that it wouldn't be possible for me to accomplish my work tasks with the same focus and vigor if I were back living far from nature.

Ultimately, I had to explore the extremes of the spectrum to balance out the demands of a high-tech career with the mental needs of my own psyche in wide open spaces.

16

TASTING THE MARROW

The yard was littered with the dead bodies of at least three yellow-bellied marmots. I slowly rolled to a stop at the end of the driveway. Curious as to what I had gotten myself into, I stepped out of my truck and made my way toward the beautiful log cabin overlooking the aspen-laden draw below.

As I got within one hundred feet of the house, I heard the door creak open, and the undeniable sound of a shotgun being racked with a round. Stepping onto the porch was a short-haired, hunch-backed woman wearing an oversized T-shirt.

"Who are you, and what do you want?" she said in a defensive tone.

"I'm Zach! I am here to help you with your bear problem," I replied.

A little uneasy, I could feel my pulse rise as her eyes squinted hard, trying to figure out who I was.

"Who are you?" she asked again.

A little louder this time, I shouted, "Zach Hanson! We spoke on the phone! You have a bear breaking into your home?"

A smile broke through her tough demeanor, and she said, "Oh, yes! Come on in and let me show you my foxes!"

Relieved, I made my way to her door and was shuffled into her home.

Sharon had been born in the little Idaho village that I now called home. Her family was brought here by mining in the early 1900s and had been involved in the town's oscillating growth cycles in one form or another for decades. Now pushing her late eighties, Sharon was the embodiment of a true pioneer woman who prided herself on self-sufficiency and grit.

As she welcomed me into her living room, I watched her place the still-loaded shotgun on the floor in front of a small shrine she kept to honor the foxes she had "befriended" over the past several decades. In an attempt to break the ice, I asked her about the dead marmots riddled with bullet holes that were strewn across her front yard.

"Ohhh, those fat bastards keep digging holes under my house, and I am afraid it's going to collapse. This house is over one hundred years old, you know?" she said, beaming with pride.

Sharon showing me where the bear had been breaking in.

Sharon was eager to talk about her foxes. She told me that she had been "taming" a family of foxes for over thirty years and would sit out on her deck to feed them on a regular basis. They all had names and were ensconced on her shelves with pictures and little fox chotskies.

She lit up and took on the glow of a twenty-something, telling me about her "pets." She naturally scooted her old body toward the shelves, and I noticed that her left foot was now covering the barrel of the shotgun that she had laid down on the floor when we first walked in. With another excited step forward toward the fox shrine, her back foot landed about an inch from the trigger well on the old gun, which likely had no safety switch.

No longer able to concentrate on the stories of her foxes, my tunnel vision was focused on her back foot. If her toes were to hit the trigger, she would blow her left foot clean off. So I stood at the ready to shove this frail eighty-pound woman away from her gun while she continued to regale me with stories of old. I was relieved when she finally stepped away to show me other parts of her living museum, as I had not been absorbing a single word while she was standing on top of her loaded firearm.

After a whirlwind tour on the history of our small town, she finally showed me the scene of the crime that I was there to help address. For the past few weeks, a large black bear had been breaking into her kitchen to steal food. This was evidenced by the broken windows, scratched door, eggshells, and bear scat that was spread across her home.

It was clear that a three-hundred-plus-pound black bear had been helping himself to a nightly buffet, all while this grizzled old lady slept alone in the next room.

In a creative attempt to ward off the bear, she had taken the time to paint her kitchen door with splotches of fluorescent neon green. She had apparently heard that bears don't like that color and wanted to give it a try, but the bear kept coming. Having given the unwelcome visitor every chance to vacate her premises, she realized she needed help, and as the new town "trapper," my name got passed along as someone who might be able to take care of the problem.

Though I had already used my bear tag for the season, I promised I would scope it out and do some recon for her. I would then have one of my friends who still had a tag in their pocket come take care of the problem for her.

Leaving Sharon's place, stepping over the massacred marmots, I began to revel in how lucky I was. I was surrounded by independent thinkers, like Sharon, who lived life on their own terms in a wild place and dealt with severe daily consequences for every action they took, with a smile and sometimes a gun.

Blood, Bones, and Water

In that thankful state of mind, I was taken back to the recent clarity of mind I'd had while riding a snowmobile at night, deep in the backcountry after a fresh snowfall. That night, I could see for miles and couldn't help but feel engulfed by the magnitude of the mountains with bright moonlight reflecting on them. It made me feel like it was daylight. When I stopped and killed my engine, the world fell completely silent, and in that moment I was truly alone.

That silence had crept into my repatriated soul as I stared off into dense pine forests. I felt my condensed breath freeze on my beard, and I could feel the kinetic violence of nature surrounding me. It was those extremes on the spectrum of life that I had needed to explore in order to find out who I was under the facade of a successful career, monotonous hobbies, and an overall neutered life. I had stripped away those trappings of modern living and inserted myself into tough everyday situations far from creature comforts. Only then was I able to evaluate who I *truly* was at my core.

I was not Zach the artificial intelligence expert, I was not the airline status I had accrued, I was not the globetrotting speaker, and I certainly wasn't the man entirely dependent on a larger apparatus to support me. I was just a walking sack of bones, blood, and water, and it was my experiences learning to hunt and trap that provided me with the connection back to where I truly came from, the earth itself.

Over those first few short years of living in the backcountry, I had been able to tie myself back to nature on a gut level, grow an amazing family in the backcountry, and plant myself in a small, tight-knit community. I believe these are the things that make up the core of who we are as a species, and the things that I had previously ignored.

Sign of Our Times

My desire to reconnect with nature wasn't isolated or unique. In fact, the COVID-19 pandemic brought light to those primal emotional needs worldwide. The realization that state infrastructure wasn't always reliable, that grocery store shelves could go empty, supply chains could break down, and heating sources could malfunction all threw a wet blanket of fear over the entire nation and world.

Whether you were an executive, a stay-at-home parent, or from any other walk of life, it was apparent that it was necessary to start to learn and practice small bits of self-reliance. Channeling that fear, I saw colleagues and friends trying to find ways to get outside more with their kids and purchase basic preparedness kits, generators, and tools. That trend in self-sustainability even extended to a nationwide uptick in urban chicken keeping, micro-farming, beekeeping, and sign-ups to personally butcher farm animals for meat.

Everyone's journey to exploring self-sufficiency was different, with some mimicking my all-in approach, while others were dabbling and running at their own pace. No path was more right than another, and it was a reflection of how we as a nation individually evaluate risk.

That type of individual risk assessment was beautifully articulated to me on one snowy Sunday, when our town's preacher spoke on that very topic. He described risk as an ever-present condition that we can never fully wrangle. That no matter where we go in life, and no matter what mitigations we put in place, there would always be unknowns that we as a people just have to accept and relinquish to a higher power.

He went on to tell us about a Canadian family who, in the late 1980s, were terrified about the threat of thermonuclear war. In an effort to mitigate that risk, the family set out on a multiyear research effort to find the safest place on earth that would give them the greatest chance of survival in a worst-case nuclear scenario.

After much deliberation, in 1981, the family moved to a small town of about two thousand people named Port Stanley. That city just so happened to be nestled in a small island chain off the coast of Argentina, which was better known as the Falkland Islands. Unbeknownst to the family, within a few months of moving to their new, well-researched safe haven, Argentina would invade those islands, and a short time later, the British and Argentinians would duke it out in a final battle that took place within a few miles of the Canadian family's new homestead, destroying it in the process.

The moral of the story is that there is no place fully insulated from the perils and risk of dependency on our modern society. You could take the route I did, move to the middle of nowhere and live a self-sufficient life, or you could take smaller steps to introduce self-sufficient habits into your family's existing structure. You may evaluate risk like Sharon, who can sleep soundly while a bear rummages through her kitchen only feet away, or be more concerned about a stranger walking onto your property. No approach is wrong or will necessarily afford you more safety and learning than the other, as long as you put in the effort to learn some baseline sustainability skills.

The important thing that my family and I personally landed on was to focus on finding daily ways to learn and preserve the practices and traditions of our ancestors. We wanted to be able to perfect the basic fundamentals of survival in order to pass those quickly forgotten skills on to our children, in the event that our broader machine one day breaks down.

As my family continues to push forward learning to live the rugged life we chose, I often go back to that fateful plane ride when I heard the life-changing words of one of my favorite fictitious mountain men, Del Gue, from *Jeremiah Johnson*. He said, "There are benefits to living in the mountains amongst the animals and savages." Now having personally tasted the marrow of the Rocky Mountains and emulated the life of my heroes, I couldn't agree more.

Made in the USA
Columbia, SC
21 October 2022

69816869R00140